# THE HEBREW ISRAELITE COMMUNITY

Edited by

## A. Paul Hare

University Press of America,® Inc.
Lanham • New York • Oxford

Copyright © 1998
University Press of America,® Inc.
4720 Boston Way
Lanham, Maryland 20706

12 Hid's Copse Rd.
Cumnor Hill, Oxford OX2 9JJ

**Library of Congress Cataloging-in-Publication Data**

The Hebrew Israelite community / A. Paul Hare, editor
p.   cm.
Chapters one, three, and four have been presented at meetings from
1993 to 1995; chapter 5 has been previously published in
Anthropological quarterly, 1996.
Includes bibliographical references and index.
1. Black Hebrew Israelite Nation.   I.  Hare, A. Paul (Alexander
Paul).
BP605.B38H43  1998  299—dc21   98-39927 CIP

ISBN 0-7618-1269-5  (cloth: alk. ppr.)
ISBN 0-7618-1270-9 (pbk: alk. ppr.)

# THE HEBREW ISRAELITE COMMUNITY

Typeset by WordByte, P.O.B. 3102, Beer-Sheva, Israel

# Contents

Ben Ammi Ben Israel
Spiritual Leader of the Hebrew Israelite Community

# Foreword

"In the world of the sociologist, as in the more secluded laboratories of the physicist and chemist, it is the successful experiment which is decisive and not the thousand-and-one failures which preceded it. More is learned from the single success than from the multiple failures. A single success proves it can be done. Thereafter, it is necessary only to learn what made it work."
(American sociologist Robert Merton, from the 1991 National Urban League Annual *State of the Race* Report.)

Initially when hearing about this book project and understanding that our Community was going to be evaluated according to certain "scientific methodologies," we had our doubts about how it might actually turn out. What we were ultimately facing was the classic debate between what is deemed the "solidly empirical" or scientific — and as a result, seemingly unquestionable — and what is commonly regarded as the ethereal or intangible, the spiritual. Each ideology and its practitioners possesses its own definite set of laws, measures, standards — a complete methodology. Quite frankly, we just did not know if it would be possible to reconcile the two.

Without question or apology, we are a spiritual movement and being spiritual men and women, we realize that the things that have been accomplished have come about specifically because of our adherence to certain spiritual, God-inspired laws or principles. Hence our concern.

Yet, upon reading the observations of Professor Paul Hare and the other writers in this work, we were more than pleasantly surprised. The writers seem sensitive to the differences between these two very different schools of thought. They took the extra effort needed to find those areas of science which might reflect what was taking place in the community, in the process, ignoring the tendency to force the results to fit the standards of measurement.

The opening quote from Robert Merton is significant because it speaks to the standard that is established by a success. Certainly by any measure, when you look at what has been accomplished by our Community in the Holy Land over the past 30 years, one would definitely proclaim it a success. Our people, having a history of subjugation in the Americas, took on the challenge of establishing a new society, refusing to base the institutions or the infrastructure upon the society which we left. We had to bring about a new reality based on our understanding of the scriptures.

Make no mistake, there is an inherent relationship between the process and the results. Our accomplishments — founded upon spiritual laws — are real, tangible and quantifiable. While some might still wish to debate that the methodology, the "empirical" truth of Merton's statement remains unchallenged.

Our objective in coming to Israel was to be a light unto humanity. In being that light, we stand to afford all men an opportunity to share in the benefits of living according to the guidelines and standards of the God of Israel.

When scientists can see the worth of this social experiment and invest the time that these scholars have to bring its reality to these pages, they will have illustrated how the scientific and spiritual can be meshed.

Ultimately, in illustrating the magnitude of our success, we feel that this work underscores the validity of the "spiritual methodology" we have applied. In doing so, the work opens another door for those who might have been inclined to only give credence on the "scientific." For those seriously in search of another understanding, it should force them to consider another way. If that takes place, then our mission has been accomplished.

*Ben Ammi Ben Israel*

# Preface

I was first introduced to the Hebrew Israelite Community in 1991 by Sister Shimia and then by many others who, in turn, took time to be interviewed and to share with me their experiences of early days and of the present life in the community. This account of community life is an introduction reflecting arrangements at the time the chapters were written. Even as the book was in production the physical structure and accommodations within the community were being improved and the social organization was undergoing change, as was the relationship with the larger Israeli society.

Sister Yadah and I have had frequent meetings over the years to draft and re-draft a document that would reflect the spirt of the community. Without her collaboration I would have had no story to tell. Ben Ammi, the Spiritual Leader of the community, has been most gracious and supportive of the enterprise. His Foreword indicates the context in which the Community has come to life and the vision that inspired it.

I would also like to acknowledge Prince Gavriel Hagadol for his spiritual insight and Minister Amadiel and Sister Zehorah for their editing skills.

Earlier versions of some of the chapters in the book have been presented at professional meetings or have been published. Chapter 1, the introduction, was presented as a paper at the meeting of the Israeli Anthropological Association (Hare, 1993b). Chapter 4, on leadership and priesthood, was presented as a poster talk at the meeting of the American Sociological Association in 1994. Chapter 3 on health care, was presented as a paper at the Association for the Sociology of Religion in 1995. Chapter 5, Israel as Africa, Africa as Israel, is reprinted by permission of the *Anthropological Quarterly,* where it was published in 1996 as part of Volume 69(4).

*A. Paul Hare*

# Chapter 1

---

# Constructing a Virtuous Reality

## A. Paul Hare

The Black Hebrews in Israel call themselves the Hebrew Israelite Community. Although there are other groups called Black Jews in the United States (cf. Berger, G., 1978; Brotz, 1964) this is the only group that has returned to the "Promised Land" of Israel. The members of the Hebrew Israelite Community are African Americans and their children, originally mainly from Chicago and Detroit. Some of the adults and their spiritual leader, Ben Ammi, were part of the more than 300 persons who left the United States in 1967, lived for two and a half years in Liberia, and moved to Israel in 1969. Most of the original group did not complete the journey and many new adults have joined the community since then in addition to the 600 children who have been born in the community. Until 1990, when there was an agreement that the members of the community would be granted American passports and visas for temporary residence in Israel and work permits, they had no legitimate status in Israel. Since they were not bona fide Jews and did not wish to convert, they were not entitled to become citizens of Israel under "the law of return." The mid-1970s were a particularly stormy period in the history of the community with verbal and physical confrontations between members of the community and representatives of the Israeli government. The largest part of the community lives in a former absorption center in the town of Dimona, which contains the communal dinning room, heath facilities, clothing work room, school, sport facilities, rooms for rehearsals for music and dance, and spaces for worship and other public events. Small groups of community members live in Arad and Mitzpe Ramon, with a few members in other areas such as Tel Aviv where the community operates a vegetarian restaurant. The current membership of the community in Israel is given in their public relations material as 2,000 persons.

Several books contain accounts of the activities of the community during its early days (Ben-Yehuda, 1975; Gerber, 1977; Lounds, c. 1981; Gavriel HaGadol, 1993). Some of the more recent events have been described in the Hebrew and English press in Israel (cf., Chertok, 1991). The religious and philosophical orientation of the community is given in four books by Ben Ammi, the spiritual leader (Ben Ammi, 1990, 1991a, 1991b, 1994) and in *The Original African Heritage Study Bible* (1993) prepared in collaboration with members of the community.

## The Community's Changing Character

Although in 1993, after the community members had been able to establish themselves in Israel as American citizens with temporary resident visas, work permits, and the provision for their children to be part of the Israeli school system, it would be easy to recognize the "utopian" aspects of the communal life, this was not always the case. An observer at an earlier period in the history of the community would have "defined" the community in a different way.

From 1963 when the first members of the community began to meet together in Chicago through 1965, the most prominent characteristic of the group would have been their formation as followers of a charismatic leader, Ben Ammi, then in his early 20s. From 1966 when Ben Ammi proposed the idea of moving to Liberia, through the "exodus" of 300 to 400 persons in 1967, and the two and one half years spent in Liberia, the group would have been identified as a part of the earlier "Back to Africa" movement. From 1969 when the first members of the community arrived in Israel through 1977 when they had predicted that the Millennium would occur following Armageddon, they would have been described as a millennial cult. When the destruction of Armageddon did not occur, community members held a spontaneous assembly during which they concluded that the Kingdom of God was already present in their community and that they should share their vision.

The early days were beset by physical, social, and political problems which were to continue until 1990. In 1978 a committee was appointed in the Israeli parliament to make recommendations concerning their position in Israel. In 1980 the committee concluded that they were not Jews, but a cult, however the committee recommended that the community be allowed to stay in Israel. The next year the main group of members of the community, who had been staying in crowded apartments in Dimona, were given the buildings of an abandoned absorption center in Dimona to rehabilitate and use as a base for their community activities.

In 1990, with pressure from African-American and other American Congressmen, they were reinstated as United States Citizens, since many had given up their passports to avoid deportation in the earlier years. They had also begun to do bio-organic farming and became a member of the Israel Bio-organic Agricultural Association. By 1992 they had been given funds by the United States to build a new school building and had the expectation of becoming permanent residents of Israel, if not citizens, within the next few years. The community was now established, with a very visible and coherent life style, and the members could now devote more energy to fulfilling their utopian purpose and mission.

## Constructing a Virtuous Reality

There are many things that could be said about any community, especially about one that brings together elements of cultures long past with those of the present and even elements that the community attempts to model for cultures of the future. This chapter will deal with one aspect of the life of the community, indicated in the title: "Constructing a Virtuous Reality." The main idea, as recorded by Berger (1963:148–9), is that society provides the language and meanings that make the world believable. "All meanings are transmitted as social processes. One cannot be human, authentically *or* inauthentically, except in society." This idea was further elaborated by Berger and Luckmann (1967:75) in their analysis of the social construction of reality:

Only through... representation in performed roles can the institution manifest itself in actual experience. .... Neither the drama nor the institution exist empirically apart from this recurrent realization.

On a visit to the Hebrew Israelite Community a first impression is formed by the specially designed clothing worn by all members that distinguishes them by age, sex, and social position. Men and boys wear knitted skull caps, large enough to cover their "Afro" hair styles, "dashiki" type shirts, long pants, and for special occasions hand crocheted "Eco" shoes made of natural materials. The fringes of the garments contain knots and threads with religious significance. Women and girls wear turbans, head ties, or other head coverings according to their age and social status, long dresses with high necklines and flowing sleeves, designed to emphasize the person rather than the body. Most of the outer clothing is designed and manufactured by members of the community in their communal sewing center.

A continuing acquaintance with the community reveals the fact that all aspects of community life, including food, health, education, economics, music, and especially religious worship, have been given a special meaning as part of an holistic approach to life. This life is to be performed daily in clearly defined roles. For them, life is a performing art.

With the advent of advances in computer graphics it has been possible to create a variety of "virtual realities" on the computer screen and in television and cinema productions. The members of the Hebrew Israelite Community are intent on creating a lifestyle that reflects the "righteousness" called for by God as recorded in the Bible. Thus they may be said to be "constructing a virtuous reality."

The idea that new meanings should be given to aspects of community life is a basic tenet of the community, not something to be left for the observations of a social scientist. Ben Ammi, has written in his book *God, the Black Man, and Truth* (1990) that the "power to define" the conditions of the life of Black people has too long been held by "Euro-Gentiles." The power to define, in the hands of evil men "is a weapon of oppression and satanic control" (Ben Ammi, 1990:56). The power to define is defined as "the ability to discern and the will to interpret and implement ideas and philosophies in order to be totally victorious in battle against one's enemy" (1990:57). This power to define, to give meaning to social events through the social construction of reality, is seen as being even more important than the power to control the actions of men and nations. Ben Ammi reaches the same conclusion as that of a sociologist of the social interactionist school. Once a set of meanings has been internalized, social control is exercised by the individual by monitoring behavior rather than because of external threat or physical control.

## Two Themes (Pro), One Theme (Con)

In constructing their virtuous reality the members of the community incorporate two themes that they view favorably, while attempting to "purge" themselves of attributes of one theme that they view unfavorably. The first favorable theme is a combination of the righteous way of life, as decreed by God in the Bible and represented by the early Israelites, together with an interpretation of Black history. This interpretation of Black history, which has been recorded in articles in *Newsweek* (January 11, 1988; September 23, 1991) and other popular publications, places the origin of humanity in the Garden of Eden in the "fertile crescent" of Northeastern Africa. Not only were the first man and woman Black, but many important figures in the Bible and in world history were Black. The Israelites' tradition is understood to have been carried westward across Africa by people who later became slaves in America. Thus some of the present-day African-Americans are seen as part of this lineage.

A second favorable theme is embodied in an holistic philosophy that brings together a vegan diet, organic farming, clothing of natural fibers, and other activities that consciously relate the activities of humanity to the preservation of the natural environment.

The theme that is viewed unfavorably is represented by the ghetto life in the United States with its alcohol, drugs, and crime, where the African-American male was often absent from family life. This theme also includes a strong stand taken in Ben Ammi's early writing (1990) against the "Euro-Gentile" who has wasted and polluted the world's environment and resources.

These themes are evident in a statement of the purpose and mission of the Hebrew Israelite Community, as prepared for a pamphlet by the community (c. 1993) entitled "Fulfilling the Vision":

> The purpose and mission of the Hebrew Israelite Community is to invoke the presence of God in the affairs of men. We realized just how far we had been led away from God and were astounded by the drastic changes required for those of us who desired to fulfil our responsibility to God as Hebrew Israelites. Nonetheless, we have committed ourselves to the high degree of courage and discipline required to establish an alternative lifestyle that is in harmony with the cycles of God. This requires the development of alternative institutions for education, medicine, social order, diet, and dress.
>
> We have been motivated by our spiritual leader, Ben Ammi, to take on the Divinely-inspired mission to establish the prophetic "Kingdom of God" in the Holy Land, and thus herald the beginning of the establishment of the long-awaited Kingdom of God on earth for all men. We have built a society based on the precepts of righteousness which emanates from the presence of God and serves as a living example for *all* men—a society where solutions to the seemingly irreversible problems that plague mankind—rampant disease, drug abuse, sexual abuse, corruption, ecological destruction, and disintegration of the family unit—can be found.

The three themes are maintained by the inspiration of Ben Ammi, and by centralized control of daily events, such as growing vegetables and fruits organically, preparing breakfast and lunch for all children in the communal kitchen and dinning room, providing clothing of a uniform style from the clothing workroom, administering health care by the community doctors, nurses, and midwives using herbal remedies, and the provision of a co-teacher in some of the classrooms in the new school to ensure the understanding and transmission of community values. All ranks of leaders in the community spend much of their time in counselling members with regard to matters of daily living. Special rituals are provided for major life events: birth, coming of age, and marriage. Special events are scheduled for days of historic or religious significance and to recognize the achievements of the "sisters," "brothers," and youth. At public gatherings a special set of young men carrying staffs or "walkie-talkies" are in evidence to protect the spiritual leader and other dignitaries and to ensure proper conduct on the part of the children.

## Righteous Community or Religious Sect?

Members of the community would insist that their way of life is "righteous" rather than "religious," since religions are man-made whereas the righteous way of life was specified directly by God in the Bible. Nevertheless, sociologists would tend to classify them as a form of religious sect. The definition of a sect can be found in many sources, for example:

A group claiming specialized leadership or teaching, a truer understanding of the scriptures, that may develop within or in opposition to an organized religion (Ferm, 1945:669), who live apart from society in some way (O'Dea, 1968:131), with a strong sense of self-identity, requiring the complete and conscious allegiance of the members (Wilson, 1970:26). They provide an answer to the question "what shall we do to be saved" and reject the orthodox way to salvation (Wilson, 1970:36–37).

Within the general category of "sect" several types have been identified. Wilson (1970:38–40) describes seven types:

(1) Conversionist — Emphasis on being born again, inner change.

(2) Revolutionist (transforming) — God will change the world and they may help. There is no joy since God is a stern judge.

(3) Introversionist — Cut off from society.

(4) Manipulationist — Better body vigor and mental ability (leading to power and wealth) is gained by supernatural, esoteric, or occult means.

(5) Thaumaturgical — Belief in a personal miracle.

(6) Reformist — Use insights from apprehension of the divine to reform society.

(7) Utopian — The world is evil because men have created an evil system. Return to the basic principles of the creator.

The Hebrew Israelite Community is closest to type seven, utopian.

Wilson (1967:17–18) has also identified five ways in which a sect may form:

(1) Around a charismatic figure.
(2) A schism within an existing sect.
(3) Individual seekers coming together.
(4) Attempts to deinstitutionalize and deritualize an existing church.
(5) Non-denominational revivalism.

Although the members of the Hebrew Israelite community were drawn from persons familiar with a Southern Baptist form of worship and were seeking their roots in the Bible and in Africa, their philosophy and their moves, first to Liberia and then to Israel, are clearly the inspiration of their charismatic spiritual leader, Ben Ammi.

## Social Structure and Communitas

If anthropologist Victor Turner were visiting the community he would have no difficulty in identifying aspects of the social structure. The clothing of community members distinguishes them by age, sex, and social position. The twelve men who constitute the Holy Council of Princes, the ten men who are Divine Ministers, and the Crowned Brothers and Crowned Sisters, all wear distinctive symbols of office. Little boys bow and little girls curtsey as adults pass. Terms of address reflect the idea that all members of the community are part of one family. Men are "brothers." Women are "sisters."

Turner would also be looking for evidence of "communitas" which he defines as (Turner, 1974:274):

> The bonds of communitas are anti-structural in the sense that they are undifferentiated, equalitarian, direct, extant, nonrational, existential, I-Thou (in Feuerbach's and Buber's sense) relationships.

Turner would find communitas in the relationship between the children and youth as they were grouped together in school classrooms before the construction of the new school as a result of limited space. Children within a three year age range were placed in the same class. Turner would find communitas in the many celebrations of the adults that in-volve instrumental music and singing where members of the audience as well as the musicians sing, clap, and dance in time with the music.

It has not been an easy task to construct a virtuous reality. The Hebrew Israelites have had a dual mission: (1) to constitute a community as an example of a lifestyle based on precepts of righteousness, and (2) to spread the word through precept and example in their musical composition, their performances of music and dance, their handcrafts, clothing, and vegetarian recipes. From 1969 until 1990 they were mainly involved with a struggle to maintain the community in Israel. Although in guidebooks, the popular press and television, and their own publications they had presented their message to the outside world, only in 1993 did they begin to concentrate on the second part of their mission.

# PART I

# LIVING THE NEW REALITY

Part I introduces the day-to-day activities in the Hebrew Israelite Community as the members live their new reality. In Chapter 2, Crowned Sister Yadah gives an overview of community life as it reflects a holistic lifestyle. In Chapter 3, Prince Immanuel and Crowned Sister Yadah join the editor in a detailed presentation of health care, a major emphasis in the community's lifestyle. Chapter 4 provides an outline of the activities of the formal leadership, including the Princes, Ministers, and Crowned Brothers and Sisters, as well as the Priesthood.

# Chapter 2

---

# Holistic Lifestyle

## Yadah Baht Israel

Dr. Tom Hyatt, a respected New York pediatrician, once said, "Good health does not pertain solely to physical fitness, it is a by-product of spiritual, social, economic and political factors as well" *(Jerusalem Viewpoint,* 4 (2): 4) Advocates and practitioners of holistic health would agree with this definition. At the same time, the most committed among thinkers realize that in this evermore compartmentalized world, a movement toward holism will provide the catalyst needed to bring about global change.

Dr. Fritjof Capra, who has written and lectured extensively about the philosophical implications of modern science, describes the perils of the fragmentation of our existence with extraordinary clarity in his book, *The Turning Point* (1983:xviii). "At the beginning of the last two decades of our century, we find ourselves in a state of profound, world-wide crisis. It is a complex multi-dimensional crisis whose facets touch every aspect of our lives—our health and our livelihood, the quality of our environment and our social relationships, our economy, intellectual, moral, and spiritual dimensions: a crisis of a scale and urgency unprecedented in recorded human history. For the first time we have to face the very real threat of extinction of the human race and of all lives on this planet. What we need then is a new "paradigm"—a new vision of reality—a fundamental change in our thoughts, perceptions, and values.... The gravity and global extent of our current crisis indicates that this change is likely to result in a transformation of unprecedented dimensions, a turning point for the planet as a whole."

Probably without realizing it, Dr. Capra has reiterated (although a few centuries later and in different words) the words of the Prophet Isaiah when he spoke thus to the Israelites, "For, behold, the darkness shall cover the earth, and gross darkness the peoples, but the Lord shall arise upon thee, and his glory shall be seen upon thee.... Go through, go through the gates; prepare ye the way of the people; cast up, cast up the highway; gather out the stones; lift up a standard for the peoples" (Isaiah 60:2, 62:10).

In his awareness of the truth contained in the prophecies and through observing the multi-dimensional crisis facing mankind today, the Anointed Ben Ammi, spiritual leader of the Hebrew Israelite Community, comments, "When so many things around you are based upon wrong, it then becomes the standard [the wrong standard]" (*God and the Law of Relativity*, 1991a:5). This knowledge has contributed to the motivation of the Hebrew Israelite Community to "...lift up a standard for the peoples" of which Isaiah spoke and the new "paradigm" called for by Capra. The guiding philosophy for their holistic lifestyle is best expressed in the words of the Anointed Ben Ammi: "The true worship of God is an entire way of life, a continuous action, from the meal you eat in the morning, to the job you work on. It encompasses your every deed and thought" (*God, the Black Man and Truth*, 1990:110).

The community's awareness is based on knowledge gained from the sacred writings recorded in the Bible. The first five books, from Genesis to Deuteronomy, provide the original set of guidelines for an holistic approach to life. Instructions were given to the Israelites for the management of their lives, including everything from the monitoring of dietary habits to setting the criteria for clothing as well as standards governing social behavior. Economic and environmental concerns were originally viewed and treated as a part of the whole social fabric.

While the holistic approach to life remains conjecture for many, this body of people is committed to maintaining a value system that has evolved into an environment void of the abuse, crimes and addictions prevalent in contemporary society. The manifestation of institutions and industries designed to meet the criteria for a conscious, stable and progressive society is the result of their God-inspired intellect. This intellect, as stated above, governs their approach to holism which includes everything from the food consumed, clothing worn, social habits and type of entertainment enjoyed by community members.

The high energy level of this living mosaic generates a constant flow of activities. On any given day you will find children running and playing freely outside in a peaceful environment void of smoking, foul language and drugs.

Teenagers play basketball in a parking lot which was converted into a court with KOG (Kingdom of God) painted boldly on the two backboards. Some of the girls spend their leisure time sitting outdoors crocheting various accessories to accent the unique clothing. At lunch time you might have to give way to a double row of 30 three-year-olds imitating a train on their way to the cafeteria.

Some of the children

A four-sided announcement board stands in the central square which advertises outings, meetings, articles of interest, up-coming lectures and seminars.

Groups of visitors being taken on a guided tour through the village is a regular sight. Television crews filming or still photographers in search of unique shots help to satisfy the curiosity of those who are not able to personally visit the village. If they happen to come on a Friday afternoon they might find a festive atmosphere in the central square which is transformed into a community marketplace with venders selling clothing, jewelry and handcrafted items as inspirational music wafts through the air. Should they come on a regular weekday morning they would see uniformed children on their way to the community "Brotherhood" school, workers going to the farm to tend the fields and bring fresh vegetables back for the entire community, goods being distributed from a collective foods distribution center, clothes being carried to and from the laundry service, or boys sweeping the sidewalks and cleaning yards around their homes before they go to school.

Their activities are not confined to regular working hours. Late at night the lights may still be on in the sewing center as the tailors and seamstresses complete projects left over from the day. Lights go on in the cafeteria daily at 4:00 a.m. to begin preparation for the next day. Every facet of life, from graduations to coming-into-adulthood ceremonies, weddings

A bride and groom and some of their attendants

and circumcisions, are all designed to positively contribute to the continued development of their holistic approach to life. The guidelines contained in the sacred writings are transferred to working, holistic practices.

## Dietary Habits

> *And God said, Behold I have given you every herb bearing*
> *seed, which is upon the face of all the earth, and every tree, in*
> *which is the fruit of a tree yielding seed; to you it shall be for*
> *food.*                                                    Genesis 1:29

As part of their system of preventive health care, community members enjoy a vegan diet. This is one way of actualizing the age-old adage, "An ounce of prevention is better than a pound of cure." It is common knowledge that many diseases are caused by the consumption of meat. The community maintains that all food consumed either enhances or diminishes one's level of health; therefore, as a preventative measure, they consume no animal products or by-products. Replacements for dairy products such as milk, cheeses, ice cream, etc., are produced from the soy bean. Almonds are also used to produce a highly nutritious, tasty milk. No white flour, white sugar, canned or processed foods are used in their diet. All pastries, cookies and cakes are made without eggs, baking powder or baking soda. Generally speaking, honey, brown sugar or dried fruits such as dates are used instead of white sugar. In order to avoid poisonous chemical additives like food coloring and preservatives, they only eat fresh fruits and vegetables.

Grains, beans, peas and seeds are also a very important part of the daily diet. Brown rice replaces white rice which has been stripped of all nutrients, soy beans and chick peas consumed once a week helps provide protein needed in the diet, and ground sesame seeds provide another source of essential nutrients for a balanced daily intake. Gluten made from whole wheat flour and tofu (soy bean curd) prepared in various delectable ways are excellent replacements for meats. Veggie hot dogs, steaklets and barbecued "twists" are just a few of the gluten favorites. Tofu made into various spreads, salads, battered or mixed in with stir fried vegetables creates added interest in the vegan diet. The best part of it all is that the food is not only tasty, but healthy as well.

Fasting one day each week and consuming only raw foods for one week (on a quarterly basis) are two additional preventive measures exercised by community members. On the day of rest, the Sabbath, they fast (except for children under the age of 12) which allows the physical body to rest and rejuvenate and, enhances spiritual growth. Variety and creativity makes the quarterly "raw week" a unique way of raising their level of health. Eating the uncooked foods coupled with three days of cleansing during this seven day period heightens the prospects for longevity.

As a part of pre- and post-natal care, a specially prescribed diet is part of an embellished program for expectant mothers. In *The High Holy and Sacred Diet* (1993:7–14), detailed explanation and instruction is given to help "retain optimum health during pregnancy and assist... in the nurturing, delivery and nursing of a well-formed, healthy baby." Expectant and nursing mothers are encouraged to eat more steamed and raw vegetables, as much organically grown foods as possible, increase dietary supplements, get adequate rest and exercise through walking daily.

## Customs

Together, the books of Exodus, Leviticus and Numbers provide the majority of the laws and ordinances given to the Israelites for the governing of their lives. Encompassed in these writings are the regulations for the worship of the Holy One of Israel; guidelines for Holy Days, celebrations and feasts as well as rules to follow in maintaining personal relationships and a stable society. The following is a sampling of the laws upon which community members have constructed their holistic reality.

> *Six days shall work be done; but the seventh day is the Sabbath of rest, an holy convocation; ye shall do no work therein: it is the Sabbath of the Lord in all your dwellings.*          Leviticus 23:3

Sunset Friday until sunset Saturday is the day of rest, or Sabbath, for the community. A Sabbath service is held on Friday evening for the adults and a children's service convenes on Saturday mornings. Except for those children twelve and under, they fast during this time for physical and spiritual rejuvenation.

The signs of spring and the advent of the first month of the Hebrew calender (Nisan [March-April]) mark their new year and the Passover celebration. The Feast of Unleavened Bread, begins a day later. Together, they also commemorate the exodus of the ancient Israelites from Egypt.

> *In the fourteenth day of the first month at evening is the Lord's passover.*          Leviticus 23:5

*And on the fifteenth day of the same month is the feast of un-leavened bread unto the Lord; seven days ye must eat unleav-ened bread.* Leviticus 23:6

Seven weeks later the feast of the "First Fruit" or the Feast of Weeks is celebrated.

*And ye shall count unto you from the next day after the sabbath, from the day that you brought the sheaf of the wave offering; seven sabbaths shall be complete.*

*Even unto the next days after the seventh sabbath shall ye num-ber fifty days.* Leviticus 23:15, 16

The memorial blowing of the trumpets is maintained:

*In the seventh month, in the first day of the month, ye shall have a sabbath, a memorial blowing of the trumpets, in holy convo-cation.* Leviticus 23:24

The Day of Atonement is the highest Holy Day of the year. It is charac-terized by a total fast for 24 hours and is the climax of 10 days of con-templation and prayer which begins with the Memorial Blowing of the Trumpets.

*For on that day shall the priest make an atonement for you, to cleanse you, that ye may be clean from all your sins before the LORD.*

*It shall be a Sabbath of rest unto you, and ye shall afflict your souls, by a statute forever.* Leviticus 16:30, 31

The Feast of Tabernacles (Succoth) is a reminder of the temporary shelters that the ancient Israelites lived in during their sojourn in the wil-derness.

*Speak unto the children of Israel, saying, The fifteenth day of the seventh month shall be the feast of tabernacles for seven days unto the LORD.* Leviticus 23:34

They maintain the laws of purification for women relative to their monthly cycle and at childbirth (Leviticus 12:2–5); the circumcision of all male children eight days after birth (Leviticus 12:3); and the wearing of only natural fabrics is based on Leviticus 19:19.

In addition to the biblically prescribed Holy Days, a number of fun-filled celebrations mark their annual calendar.

*New World Passover* is celebrated in mid-May to commemorate their exodus from the land of their captivity. Guests, friends and family gather for two festive days of picnicking, games and sports events. The second day is always culminated by a major theatrical presentation or a musical concert.

*International Sisters Day, International Brothers Day and Youth Day* are all occasions when community members host guests and visitors to share their philosophy and various aspects of the vibrant culture through seminars, forums, displays, clothing exhibits, musical performances, etc.

*The Holy Jerusalem Writers Conference* is open to the public and provides a forum for discussions and presentations on various subjects such as geo-politics, history and religion. A tour of various historic sights in Israel is also included within the framework of the conference.

## Economics

The guidelines contained in the sacred writings provide the basis of the community's economic system, another facet of the inter-related, holistic approach. In Numbers 26:54 Moses set the standard for the dividing of the inheritance or proportioning of land upon entering the Promised Land:

> *To many thou shalt give the more inheritance, and to few thou shalt give the less inheritance: to everyone shall his inheritance be given according to those who were numbered of him.*

Provisions were to be made for the less fortunate as written in Leviticus 19:9, 10:

> *And when ye reap the harvest of your land, thou shalt not wholly reap the corners of thy field, neither shalt thou gather the gleanings of thy harvest.*
>
> *And thou shalt not glean thy vineyard, neither shalt thou gather every grape of thy vineyard; thou shalt leave them for the poor and: I am the Lord your God.*

Looking beyond the words recorded on the page, the guiding principles speak to the need for assuring that just provisions are made for *everyone*. The larger families were to receive a larger allotment of land, based on need, and the land owner was to leave a portion for the poor and sojourners to glean.

This guiding principle provided the basis for the community's economic system of "all things in common" whose first priority is to assure that everyone's fundamental needs are met and that no one goes without. In keeping with the scriptural guidelines, one individual may be a doctor who has training and skills that required many years to acquire and has a wife and two children. Another may be a street sweeper with a family of nine. According to the system of all things in common, the community would ensure that the man with the larger family received more because he had the greater need. There is a communal sharing and, above all things, a communal concern for the common man.

Food is purchased and bills are paid collectively. Everyone pays a percentage of their earnings into a central economic fund; however, contrary to socialism, private ownership is permissible. Their concern is to maintain an economic system which is able to balance the concept of private ownership with meeting the needs of the whole. It is also paramount to them that as this system develops, it will not foster waste and over-consumption. One of the ways they accomplished this goal is through their collective sharing of facilities and the economic responsibility for maintaining them.

Ninety percent of their clothing is made in their community sewing center where the sewing machines and other related appliances are shared. Skills are also shared. Since the majority of the sewing is done there, everyone benefits from the professional expertise in all aspects of clothing design and manufacture.

The communal cafeteria serves over 600 children breakfast and lunch meals six days a week. This is the enactment of the initial stage of a plan which, when fully activated will serve adults as well as children all their meals every day.

In addition, laundry service is available six days a week.

"The House of Life" is a natural child-birthing center. An accomplished staff of midwives, believed to be the most experienced in the world, have delivered more than 700 babies since 1971, in accordance with biblical law. After birth the mother and newborn spend their first two weeks in this facility. Her meals are prepared, served and her laundry and other tasks are done for her while she focuses exclusively on bonding with her new baby and regaining her strength. The meals the mother receives in the House of Life are completely vegan, prepared with organic fruits and vegetables grown by the community to ensure that she receives the most nutritious meals possible.

The on-premises "Conquering Lion of Judah" health spa is available for community members to utilize an array of equipment, participate in exercise classes, enjoy the sauna and Jacuzzi as well as receive massages.

In addition to the advantages of the collective, holistic lifestyle already named, community members have created cottage industries and businesses which are a part of their collective economic development plan.

Exercise class

The Community Agricultural Project's organically grown food is certified by the Israel Bio-organic Agricultural Association. The produce is distributed within the community as well as marketed throughout Israel. Their expert agriculturists have also participated in various international conferences and forums on organic agriculture, its future and how it specifically relates to labor intensive farming for rural developing areas.

"Nature's Gate" factory produces non-dairy soy milk and a line of products made from the soy bean, including tofu and a variety of delicious ice cream flavors. A number of tasty foods are also made from whole wheat flour gluten.

L'Kiem is a very unique, totally vegan food restaurant franchise in Israel whose beginning was marked in Israel in 1996. The community also has restaurants called "Soul Vegetarian" in some of the major urban areas in the United States—Chicago, Atlanta and Washington, D.C. The 1996 "Veggie Guide Atlanta" says: "'Soul Veg' as the restaurant is affectionately called for short, has found its niche as a popular meeting place for a wide range of people, from politicians to college students. It is a full-service restaurant staffed with friendly servers. Talented chefs in the kitchen and scrumptious recipes combine to make visiting Soul Vegetarian an unforgettable dining experience."

Hebrew Commerce is a wholesale food distribution company which provides most of the items required for the community's special vegan diet. The company also markets their goods to the general Israeli public as well.

Two clothing businesses, TOFLE and FOCUS, manufacture the unique cultural attire of the community. TOFLE has been featured in major Israeli publications including *Moniteen* and *Laisha.*

In Israel, "Boutique Africa" is an on-premises outlet for TOFLE, FOCUS as well as many of the hand-crafted items made by community members. In the U.S. there are boutiques in each of the cities where the community has extensions.

These businesses were specifically developed with the dual purpose of contributing to the economic base of the community while exposing the public to positive, holistically designed alternatives.

## Clothing

Clothing is a cultural trademark and an immediate means of identifying a people. Chinese women are known for kimonos, the Scots for kilts, sombreros are unique to Mexico and wooden shoes belonged to the Dutch.

The theme of the book of Leviticus is "holiness" and how the redeemed people should worship their God. It repeatedly refers to the Israelites' call to be a Holy people, to set a new standard. And the renewed morals were to be applied to their dress as well. Numbers 15:37–40 reads:

> *And the Lord spoke unto Moses, saying,*
>
> *Speak unto the children of Israel, and bid them that they make them fringes in the borders of their garments throughout their generations, and that they put upon the fringe of the borders a /cord/ of blue:*
>
> *And it shall be unto you for a fringe, that ye may look upon it, and remember all the commandments of the Lord, and do them;*

*and that ye seek not after your own heart and your own eyes,*
*after which ye used to /play the harlot/;*

*That ye may remember, and do all my commandments, and be*
*holy unto your God.*

Ankle-length dresses and skirts, with fringes and cord of blue at the
hem, are a part of the non-provocative clothing code maintained by the
women and girls. The males of the community also wear the fringes and
cord of blue on their shirts. The array of beautiful colorful, eye-catching
clothing worn by community members illustrates the great pride and plea-
sure they derive from being in concert with the will of God as expressed in
Leviticus. This morally sound manner of dress lends credence to the fact
that morals and style are compatible in the creation of clothing. Additionally, the absence of skin-tight jeans, high heels, see-through tops, false
fingernails and eyelashes, makeup and the like allows the natural beauty
and femininity of the females to be appreciated.

Because of the unique nature of the community's cultural dress, they
make their own from natural fabrics only—cotton, silk, wool and linen.
The benefit of the holistic approach is epitomized in this instance because

Community sewing center

the wearing of natural fabrics eliminates the potential health hazard presented by wearing synthetics which has been linked to various skin diseases and cancer. Thus, the wearing of morally sound clothing made from natural fabrics increases prospects for health and longevity.

Within the community distinctive lines are drawn for different categories of clothing. There are no uni-sex styles. Each garment is clearly designed for either a male or female, according to Deuteronomy 22:5,

> *The woman shall not wear that which pertaineth unto a man,*
> *neither shall a man put on a woman's garment; for all that do so*
> *are abomination unto the LORD thy God.*

In returning to the "old path" of the forefathers, younger daughters do not wear their bigger sisters' or mothers' clothing. Each age group has its own style. Even in the school uniforms, the styles change according to age level, in color and design. The younger girls wear a simple jumper while older girls wear a two-piece garment. Before the age of sixteen the only type of hair covering that girls can wear is a simple "fall" (scarf). After sixteen the girls can wear a variety of head wraps or turbans (after school) as the women do to accent their outfits. Between the years of eighteen and twenty, after entering into adulthood, the young women begin to wear appropriate styles.

## Music

Music plays an important role in the community and in the relationship of the community to the society-at-large.

Quoting from the writings of the Anointed Ben Ammi in *God, the Black Man and Truth* (1990:32, 34) he says,

> *Music is much more than a form of entertainment; music iden-*
> *tifies races, nationalities and communities. It has far-reaching,*
> *hypnotic effects on the brain and soul, and can take complete*
> *control of the body and mind. Music can determine the mood of*
> *a person or a people. After comprehending its profound effects*
> *on the mind, it stands to reason that we must beware, for the*
> *effects can be good or evil. Music is like a series of thought waves*
> *that cause men to think and do right or wrong, wise things or*
> *foolish things. In addition to that, there are sounds that destroy*
> *ear drums, shatter light bulbs, and crack glass. We must also ask*
> *ourselves: is there a mode or musical sound that can destroy the*

*mind? The answer is certainly yes.... In our quest for God, we
must bring forth a righteous sound upon the instruments; we
must halt the onslaught of music that weakens and destroys.*

Believing that it would be inconsistent to overlook the importance of
the influence of music while setting this new standard, members of the
community create music which is designed to inspire people to think, feel
and do the right things. For them, the highest form of musical expression
is to praise the Holy One of Israel through the different styles of music
they perform such as gospel, jazz, reggae, etc.

*Praise him with the sound of the trumpet; praise him with the
psaltery and harp.*

*Praise him with the timbrel and dance; praise him with stringed
instruments and flutes.*

*Praise him upon the loud cymbals; praise him upon the high
sounding cymbals.* (Psalms 150:3–5)

This is the goal of community musicians—to influence their audi-
ences through positive sounds that praise God and provide inspiration.
In doing so, they are fulfilling their call to come forth and once again "play
the Word of God."

In the earliest stages of the development of bands in the community
the major focus of the musicians was to make money. There was no concern as to how the music would effect peoples' lives. There was no consideration of the meaning of the words. Each song simply described an episode in someone's life: you got your man or your man left you. Even with
gospel music there was no feeling of the depth of touching someone's
soul. Once the musicians were made aware of the teachings according to
the laws of God it was possible to focus on what one could do to reach the
souls of man. As one became able to understand the Godly mind it was
possible to write songs that would help others understand the Godly mind
and to awaken them to the need for righteousness.

The musicians now had a purpose, they were no longer just entertainers. All of the Divine Minstrels have come to realize that their purpose
and mission is to educate, uplift, and to inspire, as well as to entertain.
This includes both songs and instrumental music. The spirit in all the
music is one of righteousness, goodness, and wholesomeness, whether it
be in the form of ballads, rhythm and blues, or reggae. Music is used in
the world today as a vehicle to influence people; therefore, music must be
used to influence people to do that which is right.

Men of the Divine Entertainers

Women of the Divine Entertainers

Being an integral part of the life of the community, music is performed at social gatherings, weddings, various ceremonies, and in Sabbath services. Each of the groups has a positive name to reflect the spirit of God. The first band formulated, the Soul Messengers was formed in the late 60s. Presently, there are three additional bands—the Sons of Light, Prophetic Destiny, the Prophets of Sound, and Tikeeah. There are male and female vocal groups, an adult choir called the New World Gospel Choir, and a children's choir.

Community musicians also perform at weddings, private affairs, and music festivals for the Israeli public. Several of the groups have received official commendations from the Israeli Defense Force for morale-boosting performances.

The musicians have been involved in a number of projects. The community contracted with Scopus Films to provide the music for a series of children's animated video films. Original scores were recorded for the films *Follow That Goblin, Follow That Sleigh*, and *Follow That Bunny*. The themes are anti-mindless technology. Another project, "Little Muscles" was created to inspire children to exercise. Community artists regularly perform with top Israeli musicians and have also been offered contracts to write and perform music for theatrical plays.

The musical, Sound!, which tells the history of the community through song and dance was well received on its American tours. A very gripping video clip was purchased for UNESCO using the New World Gospel Choir singing "Ruanda." A combination of Prophetic Destiny and Tikeeah captivated the audience while performaing inWest Africa.

## Education

Since the early 1970s community members have worked to develop an educational institution that fosters intellectually astute adults to maintain the standards of their holistic society guided by righteous precepts.

Children of the original arrivees were accepted into the Israeli public school system. But after political problems began to develop surrounding their status, the children were denied admission to the local public schools. Thus, community members tackled the challenge of educating their children themselves. A nucleus of experienced, accredited administrators and teachers established the Kingdom School in Holiness. They took full advantage of the opportunity to incorporate subject matter which would support their value system.

Two decades of self-determined education proved to be an invaluable experience when the time came to open the doors of the Brotherhood School in September 1993. The opening of the new accredited school was a major accomplishment for the community in general and for the children specifically. The period of the 70s and 80s saw students being educated in homes, bomb shelters and under shade trees. There had been no financial backing for a formal structure nor all the necessary equipment. Today, the 22 classroom accredited school accommodates over 500 students from kindergarten to 12th grade with a 35 member salaried teaching and administrative staff. The development of the school has not progressed without challenges. The current structure is a clear illustration of how dreams are realized through hard work.

The foremost avenue for post-secondary and continuing adult education within the community is The School of the Prophets at Jerusalem. It was founded in 1974 as a support system for the holistic lifestyle and philosophy of the community. Its goal is to produce intellectuals who can balance academic and technological knowledge with the will of God as expressed by the inspired Biblical prophets. Fortified with such knowl-

Community leaders at school dedication ceremony

edge, the graduates of The School of the Prophets are able to take an active, responsible role in teaching the fundamentals of a lifestyle which is socially and environmentally sound.

The structure of the institute includes a Headmaster/Dean, administrators, teachers and "Spiritual Investigators" (post-graduate researchers.) There are five major divisions* in the School of the Prophets:

1.  Education;
2.  Priesthood;
3.  Preventive Medicine and Healing;
4.  Geo-politics;
5.  History;
6.  Economics; and
7.  Organic Agriculture and Environmental Studies.

Special courses are offered in other areas of study according to the demand. In addition to the specialized studies all students participate in periodic lectures, forums and presentations on various significant events which impact upon the world and its inhabitants.

Another continuing education option for young adults in the community is the Work/Study Program. This program offers them the opportunity to broaden their life experience and learn various skills through on-the-job training in different extensions of the community in the U.S. and Africa.

---

* Each division of study is labeled *"Divine,"* meaning pleasing in the eyesight of God.

# Chapter 3

## Emphasizing the Holy in Holistic Health Care

### A. Paul Hare, Immanuel Ben Yehuda, and Yadah Baht Israel

Health has become a major focal point in everyone's life today. Doctors, scientists and researchers continue to search for solutions to the rapid expansion of debilitating and terminal diseases such as cancer and aids.

Health care in the community is based on the premise that "An ounce of prevention is worth a pound of cure." In the life of the community this is translated into a system of preventative health care which embodies the principle that proper diet, adequate rest and regular exercise can produce a higher standard of health which will drastically reduce the need for medical care as it is known today.

The rates of diabetes, heart problems, high blood pressure, etc. is at epidemic proportions in the African-American community in America. In almost 30 years not one member of the community has had a heart attack.

The health program is a holistic preventive method. It includes reflexology, homeopathy, and chiropractic healing, but with the emphasis on following the laws of God. To maintain a healthy mind and a healthy body they feel that it is imperative to live from the sources from which we were created.

The use of various products that might be hazardous to health are monitored. The ultimate objective of the community is to use only natural fibers. Therefore the use of "pampers" as diapers for babies is discouraged.

Even though there are various schools of alternative preventive medicine the community in Israel is the only group of African-Americans who practice such a system of health care as a part of a holistic lifestyle.

Community members believe that health is the manifestation of the true worship of God in body, mind, and soul in its entirety. Whereas sickness, disease, and death are the result of violations and rebellions against the omnipotent laws of God and His creations.

## Vegan Diet and Nutrition

Included in the lifestyle of the community is a diet that is strictly vegetarian with no meat or animal products. The community members have been vegetarian for more than twenty years. The diet includes fruits, vegetables, nuts, seeds, and grain. The diet goes back to the Bible, in Genesis Chapter 1 verse 29, where the original diet was given without meat.

> *And God said, Behold, I have given you every herb bearing seed,*
> *which is upon the face of all the earth, and every tree, in which is*
> *the fruit of a tree yielding seed; to you it shall be for food.*

In the early days of the community it was a process of dropping or adding one thing at a time. Now the diet is completely vegetarian, there are no animal products or byproducts in the diet. Milk and cheese are produced from the soybean, the main source of protein. Sesame seeds also play a very important part in supplying calcium and protein. They have developed the "High, Holy and Sacred Diet" which gives the guidelines for the basic diet for the average person.

There is also a diet for expecting mothers and nursing mothers. Expectant mothers are given this diet throughout their pregnancy and during the two or three years that they may be nursing their child. Newborn babies are nursed for at least five months. They have nothing but mother's milk. After five months they are introduced to solid food. Small children, from five months to three years, are on a special program where their diet is designed to give them a good foundation for health. The children are watched closely to make sure that they are receiving all the nutrition that they need.

Maintaining the diet is easier for the children since they are given two meals a day, breakfast and lunch, in the common dining room. The evening meal is eaten in their homes. In a survey of the children's teeth a few years ago, it was found that all children born in the community up to ten years of age had no cavities in their teeth. One reason is that white sugar is not used and use of brown sugar is monitored. Honey and natural fruits are also used for sweetening. When children ask for money to buy candy, they are encouraged to buy nuts or dates. Community members make their own candies, using carob instead of chocolate.

Along with the regular food there are supplements that are recommended for everyone. The supplements include, sesame seeds, wheat germ, blackstrap molasses, parsley, kelp, and fenugreek.

Every week there are "no salt days" when no salt is added to the food. Every three months the adults of the community observe a "raw week" when they do not eat any cooked food.

Visitors to the community learn about the vegan diet. Demonstrations of the preparation of vegetarian foods are given for groups outside the community. A restaurant in Tel Aviv, run by members of the community, serves vegetarian food and sells tofu, tofu ice cream, and other vegetarian foods. The community has also published a cookbook that includes a variety of recipes for vegetarian dishes.

## Organic Farming: Community Agricultural Project

The Community Agricultural Project is a labor-intensive agricultural undertaking. The project originated from the experience gained in growing food in the community gardens. As a result of efforts there, they were able to expand, in 1987, to lease ten dunams of land for an experiment with organic agriculture in field conditions. This is a labor-intensive work wherein most labor, including seeding, weeding, harvesting, and cultivation is done by hand. The community is totally involved in the project: men, women, sons, and daughters. A dozen workers are transported to the fields from the community on a weekly basis.

From 1987 through 1997, they have expanded their efforts from 10 dunams of land, to 22 dunams of land on one moshav (collective agricultural settlement). During this period they became authorized organic growers as part of the Israel Bio-organic Agricultural Association (IBOAA). This means that the food and fields are legally certified as organic. They received certification after working the fields for three years, making sure that all chemical residues were exhausted in the soil, and building the soil through appropriate organic agricultural methods and the application of Biblical laws and cycles that govern the cultivation of the soil.

They now have access to all of the organic agricultural movements in Israel as well as networking with international organizations.

They use the drip irrigation method, that was developed in Israel, because the community is located in a semi-arid region in the Negev desert. They installed their entire irrigation system. There are irrigation specialists in the community who learned irrigation drip-system technology through on the job training. This technology is a very efficient system, in terms of utilizing the water and fertilizing. Not only is the water dripped close to the plant, but plants can be fertilized and watered at the same time using an irrigation tank. This is called "fertigation" since fertilizing is combined with irrigation.

One of the reasons why the community members are able to produce such a large quantity of food from a small area of land is because they adhere to the Biblical statutes that preserve the fertility of the soil in conjunction with intensified planting methods. As a result, their yields are increased 3-4 fold, having produced up to 200 metric tons of vegetables from their fields.

## Physical Fitness

The purpose of the community "fitness" program is to improve the physical fitness, health and longevity of the members. Their ancestors lived for many years and they believe that it can be done again. They note that the fast foods and quick way of living of today has created problems so that the life span has become 72 years for a man and 79 years for a woman. They believe it should be possible to live 150 years and upwards if they take care of their bodies correctly. The lifestyle is based on being as healthy as one can be. It requires proper diet, proper rest, and proper exercise.

They think of physical fitness in terms of four elements: 1) strength, which is the ability of the muscles to produce force; 2) muscular endurance, the power that is repeated for a period of time; 3) cardio-vascular endurance, force applied for a long haul, which means the capacity of the respiratory and the circulatory systems to supply oxygen and nutrients to the muscular cells so that activity can continue for a long period of time; and 4) flexibility, the range of movement in the joints. Attention is given to these four elements in all their physical fitness activities including sports training. The health center assists in each one of these areas to enhance longevity.

Exercise at least three times a week is encouraged, including floor exercises. For example, some members have a program of running on two days a week, a visit to the sauna on one day, and using the exercise equipment on two days for muscle toning. They believe that exercise is helpful if it increases the circulation of the blood so that the blood can continue to move and purify the body and maintain the action of the heart.

Since the Health Center is an indoor facility it can be used in all seasons. It provides a supplement to the physical fitness program of the school children, although only persons 15 years and older are allowed to lift weights.

Posted at the Health Center are helpful hints for proper diet. They realize that eating properly goes along with the exercise. The health program stresses health rather than beauty, although, for them, beautiful is healthy.

Each year, in May, two days of athletic contests are held for members of the community and their Israeli neighbors as part of the "New World Passover" celebration, organized by those in charge of the physical fitness program. The contests include track events and team games.

The community professional basketball team is called "Big Red." They play against other teams all over Israel. The community also has softball teams for both men and women, and a soccer team. Volleyball is a popular game within the community. Dancing is also included as a good form of exercise as are "Afrobics."

For community members, exercise is important to remove the toxins from the body and to help a person live life abundantly. They recognize the importance of the correct spiritual state of mind for the eradication of illness. If the mind is laden with negative thoughts and misgivings, then it is difficult to improve a deteriorating physical ailment. Thus, they feel it is important to have a joyful community since one is not only dealing with a body but also with a mind. The mind must be as free from stress as possible. This joyful mindset is shared with anyone coming into the community.

## Natural Childbirth

The community has its own pre and post-natal clinic. Mothers who have conceived are examined, beginning with the early months of pregnancy. The initial examination is followed by monthly clinic visits, up to the seventh month of pregnancy. After that the mothers come to the clinic every two weeks until the birth of the child. Classes prepare the mothers for delivery and teach them how to take care of themselves during pregnancy. The mothers also attend the pre-natal clinic in the town outside the community. So there is a dual record of the mother.

In the pre-natal program mothers are encouraged to take a brisk walk for about thirty minutes early in the morning. On returning home she has a beverage to drink and one hour later breakfast. Full basic meals are recommended for the mother, a well rounded vegetarian diet. The mother is advised to have cereal for breakfast one day, alternating with fruit the next, and steamed vegetables and raw salads for lunch. The dinner meal is eaten with her family. Mothers are advised to follow a strict diet, but she has the option to follow her own tastes. Experience has shown that if she adheres to the diet she is given she has a healthier baby.

Mothers are advised to rest between the hours of two and four in the afternoon and to retire at ten in the evening. During the months of pregnancy the mother has weekly sittings with a priest when the scriptures are read to her. Thus the baby is exposed to the word of God before birth.

The "House of Life" where babies are delivered has a staff of twelve persons, eight of whom are midwives. The mothers remain in the House of Life for two weeks after the delivery. Everything is taken care of for her: clothing is washed for the baby and the mother, meals are prepared, and rooms cleaned. The mother's basic needs are taken care of so that she can concentrate on her own health and taking care of her baby.

During the delivery process the midwife is in attendance, and if the mother so desires her mother and friends can be there. Seven persons are allowed in the delivery room, including the mother. The baby is born hearing the word of God. A priest sits outside the delivery room reading from the Bible or singing hymns of praise to God. After the baby is born and all the necessary things have been done, the baby is blessed by the priest. According to the biblical laws, if a male child is born, the child is circumcised on the eighth day by a priest.

After the mother is discharged from the House of Life, she goes home where sisters from the community continue to care for her and her family. She still maintains the Biblical restrictions of 40 days after the birth of a boy or 80 days after the birth of a girl when she must rest and is not able to do anything for her family. She continues to recuperate from the childbirth and devotes her time to the new baby. A postnatal exam is done four weeks after delivery and a return visit at seven weeks after delivery. From then on the mother comes back monthly to have the baby checked during the first year of life.

As noted above in the description of the diet, as a standard, the babies are totally breast fed until the age of five months after which time food is added. Along with the vegetarian diet, the mothers receive certain supplements, including brewer's yeast, kelp, sesame seeds, black strap molasses, and fenugreek (an herb containing minerals and vitamin B12).

The mother has prenatal examinations so it would be known ahead of time if the mother would need a Caesarian birth or if there would be other complications because of the position of the baby. In these cases the mother goes to the hospital in Beer Sheva. Also, if there are unexpected complications at the time of birth, the mother is taken to the hospital. The vast majority of the babies are delivered in the community.

There have been several twin births in the community. Babies have been born in the community weighing up to twelve pounds, however the average birth weight is the normal seven and one-half pounds.

When members of the community left America in 1968 and moved to the interior of Liberia they expected to care for themselves. Babies were delivered at the local hospital which was about thirty five miles away. On one occasion there was an emergency when the mother was not able to make it to the local hospital and the baby was delivered in the community.

Babies have been delivered in the community since 1972. When members of the community first came to Israel in 1969 the mothers went to the hospital in Beer Sheva to deliver their babies. In 1971 some were questioned about their right to use the hospital as did other immigrants. One of the mothers decided that she wanted to have her baby delivered in the community. This proved to be feasible, and the first delivery in the community took place in September, 1972. By 1996 over six hundred babies had been delivered in the community. The children receive an annual medical examination and there are regularly scheduled clinics for babies and mothers.

## Healers and Herbal Medicine

Anyone who is not feeling well can make an appointment to see one of the healers at any time. There are seven female healers who treat the women and five male healers who treat the men, although any healer may provide treatment if there is a special need. The community has taken the profit motive out of healing. The healers receive no fee for services. They do their work out of concern for their brothers and sisters.

They consider a healer as an instrument serving God with a God mind. The healer is a messenger of mercy to the afflicted. Not only must the healer excel in keeping others healthy but also must be a perfect example of health. The healer seeks to preserve the life that God has imparted by assisting nature's work of healing. The healer is also an educator teaching the right methods. Finally, for them, the healer stands as a guardian of both physical and moral health.

Herbs are used as a means of prevention and for healing, instead of the manufactured pharmaceutical products. The community healers are well versed in the use of herbs found in Israel and throughout the world. They are continually testing new remedies. Some of the healers specialize in pharmacology and prepare tinctures, ointments, and cough syrups.

Since so many diseases start in the stomach the healers have developed mild colon cleansers for everyone to use on a regular basis, so that elimination is regular. They believe that the blood is the life of the flesh. If one does not have proper elimination so that toxins and bacteria accumulate in the digestive system, the toxic waste is reabsorbed into the blood stream. Over a period of time this can develop into all types of illnesses, ranging from colds, to tumors, to cysts, to eventually cancer. The healing principal is based on the cleansing of the blood, since no disease can exist in a clean blood stream. The air, the environment, and the food one eats is full of germs, but when the body has a clean and healthy blood stream it has the ability to fight off disease.

If anyone does require the services of conventional medicine and is taken to the hospital, or even to a doctor outside the community, then one of the community healers accompanies the patient. The community healer not only comforts the patient but also acts as a liaison between the patient and the hospital or outside medical service. They serve to balance the application of community medicine with that provided by the outside source. If a stay in the hospital is deemed necessary, the healers take turns so that there is someone with the patient twenty four hours of the day. Vegetarian meals are taken to the patients in the hospital.

# Chapter 4

## Leadership and Priesthood

### A. Paul Hare

This chapter provides an introduction to the types and duties for the leaders of the community, especially the religious leaders who form the priesthood. The information is based primarily upon interviews with members of each type of leader against a background of visits to the community over a period of two years and a reading of books (Ben Ammi, 1990, 1991a, 1991b, 1994; Gavriel HaGadol, 1993) and other materials written by members of the community, including their own published version of the Bible and a booklet entitled "100 Amazing Facts on the African Presence in the Bible," as well as books and articles in the press and from other sources.

## Leadership

There are three levels of leadership in the community, the Princes, Ministers, and Crown Brothers and Sisters. They are responsible for administration, counsel, and overseeing the functions of other internal organizations. The ultimate head and spiritual leader of the community is Ben Ammi.

In the early days of the community in the United States very little was known about leadership. There was little unity within the group of leaders. After members of the community had moved to Liberia and then on to Israel the leadership became much stronger. The leaders give all praises to the God of Israel since they believe that all leadership stems from God. Theirs is a spiritual leadership. They say that this is not the way that the term "leadership" is generally understood in the outside world. The leaders are not competing with each other. They know that they have to work in order to remain servants in the Kingdom of God. The greater the servitude, the greater the leader. Ben Ammi, as the anointed leader, is recognized as the greatest of them all. The offices held by the three levels of leadership, the Princes, the Ministers, and the Crown Sisters and Brothers are respected by the community as a whole.

For the Black Hebrews the most important element in leadership is order. This order has created a sense of strength and also of pride. They assert that if there is no order in the community, even in one's home, everything would be in disarray. The leaders base their understanding of order on the order demanded by the God of Israel, as it is written in the scriptures and they strive to maintain that order. For example, within the community the Sabbath day is one of the holiest days of all. The laws that pertain to the Sabbath are maintained to the utmost. By fulfilling the law the members of the community feel that they have been strengthened.

The Princes were chosen by Ben Ammi. The Princes must continue to exhibit the same spiritual qualities of service that led to their being chosen in order to continue to hold their position. The love and respect of the community members for a Prince will determine the length of his stay in the office. The reward for a Prince is not financial, but the realization of an inner peace and an inner fulfilment by working for God to establish God's Kingdom.

There are twelve Princes, Ben Ammi is the thirteenth Prince. The Princes, sitting as a body known as the Holy Council, make decisions about the very hard problems that cannot be solved at the lower levels of the community leadership. A decision can be made by those Princes that have met at a particular time, the agreement of all twelve is not required. The twelve Princes maintain a direct liaison with Ben Ammi.

According to the talents of the Princes, some may have special responsibilities, for example, as an ambassador for the community in international relations, or as someone to turn to for consultation and counselling. However the main function of the Princes is to provide spiritual guidance for the community.

The Princes are the foundation of the community. Over the years they have done, and continue to do, everything that other people do now, from physical work to singing in the choir. They have evolved to become the spiritual guides. Because of their service to the community they were appointed as Princes. They are the Patriarchs, the pillars of the community. They began with nothing and created something. Their faith and guidance have brought the community to its present state. Thus there may be new generations of Princes, but the Princes of this generation will always remain the Patriarchs.

The second order of leadership in the community is that of the Ministers. Their portion of the leadership is to return the people unto God. God stands for that which is right. Right stands for that which gives life and that which procreates life. They help and guide the people in their daily lives. They help to maintain and promote a standard of life that will not only insure the survival of the community but also universal survival. They teach respect of the past as recorded in the Bible and how to prepare for the future according to Biblical prophecies. In the present, they are concerned with the daily welfare of the people of the community with regard to food, clothing and shelter. There are eleven ministers. They say that they differ from the leadership in the world in that they have a true global and universal concern for the survival of this world and universe. Leaders in the world are more concerned with their own area, their own community, and their own personal wellbeing and materialistic gains. Ministers oversee different areas of community life such as security, building and maintenance, agriculture, education, health, and economics.

The third order of leaders are the Crowned Sisters and Crowned Brothers. They are persons who have been taught and learned to excel in all the functions of the community. To become a Crowned Sister or Crowned Brother one must first learn the virtues of being an adult and the responsibilities of one's profession, and to coordinate these with the responsibilities in the home and community. Sisters and Brothers need to be able to motivate people, to make responsible decisions, and to always be in touch with the people. To make responsible decisions they must have a spiritual discernment as well as a knowledge of physical facts. Crowned Sisters and Crowned Brothers are chosen as leaders because they are seen to have earned the respect of the members of the community through service.

One of the main duties of a Crowned Sister or Crowned Brother is to counsel. This includes teenage counselling, pre-marital counselling, marital counselling, group counselling, and counselling at all levels. They provide a liaison function with every area of community life. They also act as advisors to various meetings and planning groups.

## Priesthood

The members of the Priesthood are men who act as mediators between God and the people of the community. They function as teachers and counselors. They circumcise the newborn male children. They read to the expectant mothers and at the time of childbirth. Engaged couples are counseled as they seek to determine their spiritual and harmonious compatibility prior to Divine Marriage. The priests explain each of the couples' roles in Divine Marriage. After marriage the priests continue as family counselors.

The piests conduct all services. On Friday evening, to inaugurate the Sabbath, a service of song, prayer, and selected scriptures from the Holy writings are read to uplift the spirit. The adults and the older children attend this service. The following morning the younger children attend a similar service designed for them. This is one of the ways that community members are assured to receive continued spiritual teachings to inspire them.

When mothers are in conception a priest reads prayers and gives teachings so that while the child is still inside the mother the mother hears the words of the priest. They believe that positive things that are heard by the mother are passed on to the child. At the time of the birth, a priest is there in the community "House of Life," along with the midwives, during the mother's labor. The priest reads and prays. At the moment of birth the priest stops reading and begins to recite the Ten Commandments, so that the first thing that the child will hear are the laws of God. This is followed by the prayer "Hear oh Israel the Lord our God is one." After the mother has settled down and the child has been cleaned, the priest comes in to the delivery room and blesses the child.

If the child is a boy, the priest knows immediately that a circumcision is imminent. The mother and child are left to rest and the priest returns in three days to check the child to see if his constitution is strong. At that time the priest determines when the circumcision will take place. The circumcision follows the prescription in Genesis, Chapter 17, beginning at verse nine, where Abraham is instructed to circumcise himself as a test of his faith to God. The circumcision is performed on the eight day. However, the child must weigh at least seven pounds before the circumcision can take place.

The priests teach as an adjunct to the school system so that there is a continuing contact as the child grows. A "Coming In" ceremony is held when the youth reaches the approximate age of twenty years. This marks the passage from childhood to adulthood. The priest teaches the youth the things they will need to know as they become adults and officiates at the "Coming In" ceremony. As young adults they are now called brothers and sisters, but they are not yet eligible for marriage. There is usually a one year waiting period before they can begin the process of "Divine Pursuit," which means that they are available to be married. If a couple admire each other and wish to be married, they can come to the priests to ask to become engaged. The priests weigh the matter. If the engagement is approved, more counselling is given by the priests. A minimum of ten sittings are held when the priest instructs the couple regarding their roles in adult life and what is expected of them according to the laws and commandments of God. All during their life in the community they are taught by the priests.

The priests acknowledge that the community does not practice religion as the world knows religion, rather a God given righteous way of life. This includes the laws, the statues, the guidelines, and ordinances. "Religion," they say, is man made. They assert that God never commanded his people to practice a religion. He commanded his people to be righteous, not religious. The priests point out that there are people in the world who call themselves religious, but this does not mean that they will not steal or kill or lie or commit adultery. If you find a righteous community, you will not find these kinds of behaviors. Religious traditions have been used to divide people, not to bring people together. The key is not to be more religious, but to be more righteous.

This approach allows the community to accept people who may be accustomed to call God by a different name in the religion they are coming from, since the righteousness of God and the love of God is truly in the heart. The main responsibility of the priests is to maintain the presence of God in the hearts of the people and to teach the people the laws and commandments of the Holy One of Israel. The community is not ritualistic. Rituals, in the very formal sense, are not practiced.

To become a priest or Cohen, a man must have it in his heart to become a priest. In the tradition of the nation of Israel the priesthood was always by birthright, the descendants of Levy. In the present day it is understood in the community that one has to have the spirit of a priest. There are no female priests. Instruction for the priesthood is given in classes in the Institute of Higher Learning in the community. A man may study the curriculum from between two and four years, depending upon his rate of advancement. After that he may be ordained as a priest.

Some priests are a part of the leadership. However, the major purpose of the Priesthood is to continually teach the law and provide guidance for the people.

The first priests were anointed in 1979. Those priests began to teach other students. There have been four graduations up to 1992. In the earlier period two of the Princes were priests. As the community began to grow there was a need for more priests. There are currently eighteen priests. They live in the three cities in Israel where there are members of the community. One priest is the Chief Administrator. An administrative council is composed of the Chief Administrator and the Administrators of all the cities. The basic organizational structure includes persons with responsibilities for communications, protocol, and other duties.

When the priests are wearing their official robes they wear a vestment that is called a "breast plate." It is emnroidered and has the symbols of the twelve tribes of Israel. A prayer shawl (shama) is worn that has a blue stripe. No one else in the community wears the blue stripe. The shawl is usually white but can be of any color. Their robes have fringes with bells and crocheted balls representing pomegranates. The breastplate represents the function of mediation between all of the people, in the early days the twelve tribes. The bell creates the holy sound as the priest moves about on sacred occasions.

# PART II

# USING THE POWER TO RE-DEFINE

Ben Ammi and the members of the Hebrew Israelite Community have not only used their power to define a new reality for themselves, but also, in the process, have re-defined some aspects of social life that have been taken as given for themselves and for others. Part II includes three examples. In Chapter 5, Fran Markowitz shows how geography has been re-defined so that Israel once more becomes part of Africa, thus merging the African and Hebrew traditions. In Chapter 6, Hagit Peres provides interviews with women to illustrate the part played by polygamy in their return to womanhood. The examples of mediation in the last chapter take place outside the community as community members help to re-define reality in conflicts of interest between African-American and Jewish Organizations in the United States, between African-Americans and Israel, between violent conflicts between African-American gangs in the United States, and between people and their environment and their God.

# Chapter 5

## Israel as Africa, Africa as Israel: "Divine Geography" in the Personal Narratives and Community Identity of the Black Hebrew Israelites

### Fran Markowitz

Ask any Israeli on which continent Israel is located and he will tell you, "Asia." Ask any Israeli to which area of the world Israel belongs, and she will say, "the Middle East." Search for the State of Israel in any World Atlas, and you will find it snuggled into the southwest bulge on maps of Asia, and as a narrow strip hugging the easternmost part of the Mediterranean Sea on maps of the Middle East. In the mass media, Israel's geopolitical existence as a focal entity in the Middle East is proclaimed and confirmed nightly by CNN and the BBC, and through hundreds of local and national broadcasts. While Israel's territorial boundaries may be contested and subject to negotiation (as is clear from the maps published in atlases and displayed in news programs that shade Gaza, the West Bank, and the Golan Heights in a different pattern from that of Israel proper), its location in the Middle Eastern portion of the Asian continent is viewed by professionals and lay people throughout the world as an obvious geographic fact.

The Black Hebrew Israelite Community, centered in the dusty desert town of Dimona, Israel, challenges this conventional wisdom by provid-

ing proof positive that Israel belongs not to Asia but to Africa. They an-
nounce through their ceremonies and in books written by their leaders
that the term "Middle East" is a capricious geographic label with no historical or Biblical connection to Israel. Instead, they proclaim that Israel is
an African land, originally populated by dark-skinned, African people:

> Prior to the excavation of the Suez Canal (1859–69) the entire Arabian
> Peninsula and what has become known today as the "Middle East" were
> connected with the African continent. African people lived and moved
> freely throughout this region of the world.[1]

> Israel was formerly composed of a Black race, just as the nations of Egypt,
> Libya and Ethiopia are comprised of Blacks....European historians, Bibli-
> cal scholars and translators conspired to disassociate Israel and Egypt from
> Africa....[2]

Whereas Martin Bernal (1987), Ali Mazrui (1986), and others have
made similar claims, the Black Hebrews do not refer to these scholarly
works to substantiate their beliefs. They find all the proof they need in the
Bible. Invoking "Divine Geography," or a way of charting the world that
"is pleasing to God,"[3] the Black Hebrew Israelites have redrawn the map
of the Eastern Hemisphere to include Israel in Africa. Thus, Africa ex-
tends west of Egypt, to include Sinai and the Arabian Peninsula, the Le-
vant, and Biblical Babylonia up to the Tigris and Euphrates Rivers—en-
compassing all the lands in which the ancient Israelites dwelled, according to the Five Books of Moses.

The following map of Africa, a key statement of Black Hebrews' identity, is displayed throughout the Community on posters and signboards,
as a framed picture in many homes, worn as pressed metal earrings and
wooden pendants, and decorates virtually every book, brochure and sheet
of paper that comes from the Public Relations Department. Its promi-
nence reflects the fact that this map is a powerful, metonymic symbol of
the Community's complex of values, beliefs, and practices. Israel as Africa, Africa as Israel presents a rightful, sacrally-endowed alternative to
the White world; it is concrete evidence that African-Americans are the
descendants of Biblical Israelites. These noble origins, discovered after
centuries of injustice when as slaves their lineage was hidden from them,
give to the Black Hebrews a legitimate base for rejecting Euro-American
racial hierarchies, White-Western[4] views of history and progress, and the
lifestyle that derives from these views.

This chapter is a consideration of how identity and knowledge are
shaped and played out within the Black Hebrew Israelite Community in
Dimona.

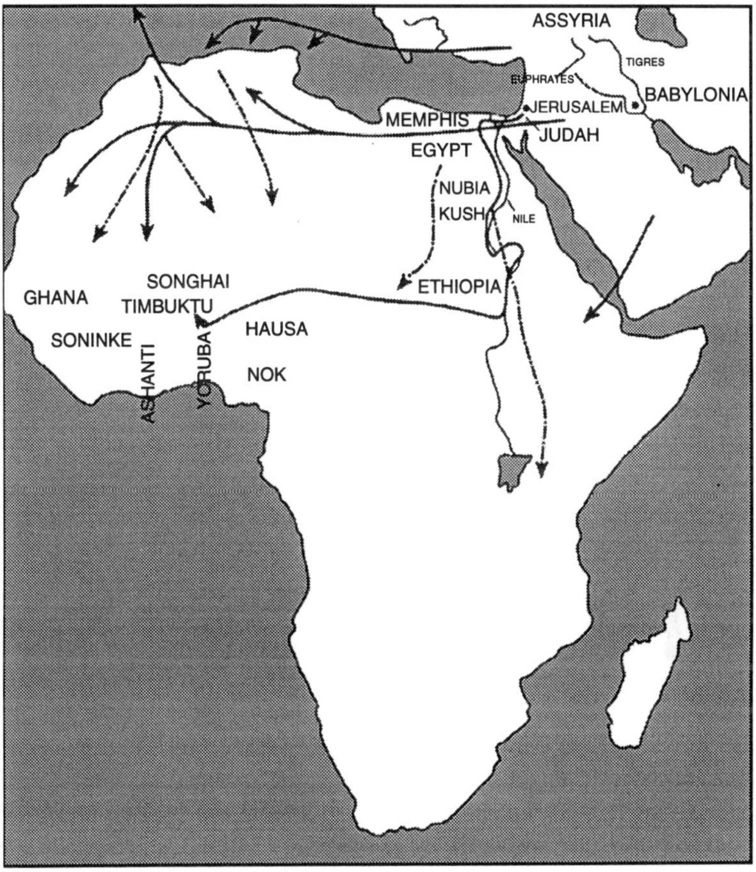

Figure 1. Black Hebrews' Map of Africa

In accordance with "the natives' point of view" it shall not portray the Community as a millennarian, revitalization, or new religious movement (cf. Linton, 1943; Wallace, 1956; Barker, 1982), but remains faithful to the Black Hebrews' own definition as a "culture, a way of life." My aim in this paper is to show through autobiographical narratives of Community members how knowledge that has been discredited, disguised, and buried can, through powerful symbols like the Black Hebrews' redrawn map of Africa, emerge to reach surface consciousness and become the catalyst for developing a counter-hegemonic social movement. I do so from the vantage point provided by Foucault's concept of subjugated knowledge (1980:81):

> A whole set of knowledges that have been disqualified as inadequate to their task or insufficiently elaborated: naive knowledges located low down on the hierarchy, beneath the required level of cognition or scientificity...a particular, local, regional knowledge, a differential knowledge incapable of unanimity and which owes its force only to the harshness with which it is opposed by everything surrounding it.

Not simply a culture of resistance (cf. Scott, 1985; Comaroff, 1985; Williams, 1991), the Black Hebrews have converted long subaltern knowledge into overt truth and practical action. Indeed, the Black Hebrews have established their own didactic orthodoxy that for 25 years has both attracted new recruits and succeeded at being a self-reproducing culture.[5] This chapter, as it explores how (former) Black Americans transform themselves into Black Hebrew Israelites by forging symbolic and actual links between Israel and Africa, demonstrates the rallying force of this culture, and why these symbolic foundations are vital to its sustenance and growth.

In order to understand the internal meanings of the Community's identity and knowledge and to transmit them to outside readers, the chapter pays close attention to the individual as volitional social actor. I shall therefore present personal narratives of several Community members, formerly African-Americans from some of the largest cities of the United States,[6] who have used their "power to define" (Ben Ammi, 1990:55–76) to extract the subjugated knowledge of their Hebraic origins and effect identity change, a radical alteration of their worldview, and a redirected lifestyle.

The chapter concludes with an analysis of the Black Hebrews' Divine Truth that Israel is Africa, and Africa Israel by considering the consequences of appropriating another people's (the Jews) central origin story to bolster their claims to a proud history. Why did they link Israel with Africa rather than strengthen identification with a precolonial African heritage and resurrect Back-to-Africa movements (see Cronon, 1955; Jenkins, 1975)? What is particularly compelling about the long written history of the Israelites that could provide the rallying force that Africa alone, and the Black Pride/Black Power movements of the 1960s could not sustain? In asking these questions I step back and challenge the Black Hebrews' "power to define" by (sadly) pointing out that even as they build what they consider to be an independent culture of resurrected knowledge, they remain bound to hegemonic definitions of and by the Eurogentile world.

# Field Methods, Fieldwork, and What Am I Doing Here?

## Anthro Standard

This chapter is based on fieldwork conducted first sporadically (1993–94) and then steadily (February-July 1995) over the period of two and a half years. My original aim was to investigate the lines of demarcation—the border zones of particular practices—that delineate the Black Hebrew Israelite Community from other Jewish Israelis. I wanted to know why the State of Israel, and all my Israeli relatives, acquaintances, and friends, refuse to accept the Black Hebrews as Jews. Along the same lines, I wished to understand why the Community calls itself a Hebraic or Judaic—but not Jewish—group, and why they steadfastly refuse to undergo conversion which would make them eligible for citizenship and full Jewish status.

I went on the Community's formal guided tour and was shown the fixtures of its Hebraic communal lifestyle: the community's Sewing Room where its head seamstress discussed the group's adherence to Biblical modesty codes and dress regulations while showing its lovely, colorful, African-influenced fashions, the Dining Room where all children receive two vegan-vegetarian meals daily,[7] and the Birth Room, where a midwife talked about natural childbirth, and the Biblical laws of purity.[8] I also attended several of the Community's major holiday celebrations and commemorative events, like New World Passover and Sisters' Day that have no equivalents in the Jewish calendar. During all these visits I was treated as a guest of honor and had little opportunity to mingle freely with spectators and participants from the Community.

Towards the end of 1994, I called my always friendly host at the Public Relations Department and told her that I was ready to begin a full-blown research project. It was to be aimed at eliciting "life stories" that would explain why individuals decided to leave behind their American lives to embrace a new identity and lifestyle in Israel. Rather than concentrating solely on practice, I wanted to learn from the practitioners themselves why they wished to break with the past to forge new lives with this Community. At the same time, it was my hope to discover through their narratives the key symbolic foundations of the Community that attract new members and sustain those who joined the group years ago.

The narratives presented in the following sections most poignantly and concisely address the links between the circumstances of African-American urban life and the search for alternatives beyond that scene that led their protagonists to the Black Hebrew Israelite Community. Of the

20 community members I spoke with, the stories of Ezriya, Adiv, Yafa, Yadiel, and Tumaya are most illustrative of the paths travelled and/or of tales of those journeys told. I could just as well have included Rakhamim's reminiscences of his upbringing in the South and his desire to "do right," Abshalom's story of searching through music, Shemaya's nagging reminder that despite her comfortable, bourgeois lifestyle that "something was missing." For the sake of brevity as well as the importance of portraying the key connections between African-Americans, Africa, and Israel, I selected those life history extracts that best embody the major routes that led to this convergence.

## The Once and Future Footnote

Before I continue on to the body of this chapter, I am compelled to take a slight detour that once was and perhaps still ought to be relegated to a footnote. This detour consists of situating me—a White Jewish Female American and new Israeli—as an uneasy fieldworker in the Black Hebrew Israelite Community.

Once upon a time, back in 1977, to be precise, I was a beginning Masters Student in Atlanta Georgia, contemplating doing ethnographic and/ or sociolinguistic research within the Black community. I decided to volunteer at the Martin Luther King, Jr. Center for Social Change to give something of myself to the community I wished to study, and to "test the waters," that is, to see if I could establish rapport. No one was ever hostile or even unfriendly to me—quite the opposite. But just about every time I walked up or down Auburn Avenue, someone, usually an elderly woman, would approach me, assuming that I was lost and point the way out of the neighborhood back into Atlanta's downtown. Recognizing that my presence was noticeable, troubling, and not wanted, I moved on to other endeavors.

These memories were piqued when I began visiting the Black Hebrews in Dimona. Well aware of their "power to define," I told this story to Crown Sister Yafa, giving her the opportunity to turn down my request for interviewing Community members. She did not. Yafa and others offered friendly cooperation with everything I have ever asked for, although sometimes I waited weeks for phone calls to be returned and began to doubt that my requests would be granted. Sometimes I felt that my efforts at individual interviews were being thwarted, sometimes I felt like I was doing research in the People's Republic of China with an official nearby at all times (see Wolf, 1985), and sometimes I reprimanded myself for being paranoid.

One balmy night, during fieldwork, I awoke with a start from a disturbing dream. In the dream I was sitting in the Black Hebrews' Guest House when in walked Crown Sister Yada, the head of the Public Relations Department, dressed in the same striking emerald green outfit I had last seen her in during New World Passover[9] when she had affirmed our friendship, embraced me and wished me well with my research. In my dream, she entered the room with her winning smile, sat down by my side and announced that my presence was no longer wanted in the Community. I asked why, had I done anything wrong? "No," she replied, "We hold the power to define."

Consciously and sub-consciously fieldwork in the Black Hebrew Israelite Community brings me face to face with the postmodern dilemma in anthropology. Intrigued with the establishment of a culture that resists minority status and invents—or, as they would prefer to say, resurrects—a culture and tradition built on the laws of the Bible and "the power to define," my goal as an anthropologist is to understand how it is that these individuals have gathered together to fight against an ideology, social structure and economic hierarchy that has demeaned and debilitated them. "I'm on your side!" I want to shout, but I dare not. My only vehicle for demonstrating sympathy and solidarity is to be a keen and committed ethnographer. Or perhaps, ultimately, to duck out from the research project altogether...but not yet.

## Knowledge, Counter-Knowledge, Self-Knowledge

The Black Hebrew Israelite Community began in Chicago during the middle 1960s, at the height of the Civil Rights movement, under the charismatic leadership of Ben Ammi. Inspired by a dream or a vision, he organized a Back-to-Africa movement in 1966, ultimately taking 300 men, women and children to Liberia to build a community of righteousness (Gavriel HaGadol, 1993: 85, 94). In 1969 he had another vision, that the group's original homeland was not Western Africa, but Eastern Africa, more specifically, Israel. Small groups entered Israel from Liberia, claiming the right to settle there according to the Law of Return.[10] The State of Israel, however, did not agree, and ever since Black Hebrews, whether from Liberia in the late 1960s, or later on directly from the U.S.A., have entered Israel on tourist visas which they simply allowed to lapse.[11] In 1986 a group of 50 were arrested and 37 deported, bringing to a climax the uneasy relationship between the Black Hebrews and the Jewish State.

Since 1992, however, after the intercession of the Black Congressional Caucus of the U.S. Congress, the two sides have made an uneasy truce; the State of Israel has granted the Black Hebrews temporary residence status, and the Community has promised to accept no new members until their status is resolved.

The Black Hebrews have also amended their self-definition over the years. During the 1970s they proclaimed in brochures and to all who were willing to listen that they were the only legitimate heirs to the Land of Israel and therefore it was part of their mission first to ignore and then to destroy the Jewish State. Since the late 1980s, this rhetoric has softened, and the Black Hebrews now acknowledge that Biblical Israel was a multi-racial society from which, after the destruction of the Second Temple in the year 70, its inhabitants fled to Europe and Asia as well as to Africa. Now their hope is to obtain Israeli citizenship and to participate fully in the life of the country (see Chertok, 1991).[12] At the 1995 New World Passover games and parade, the Israeli flag was flying along with the Community's colors.

Whether or not Ben Ammi originally intended that a permanent home for his followers be in Liberia and only happened upon the Israeli option after realizing the hardships of life in the African bush is irrelevant to the Community. Prince Rakhamim [Rockameem], echoed by Agriculture Minister Yadiel, averred that Ben Ammi all along planned to take the group to Israel but only after a stint in Liberia so that "We could return to the Land[13] the same way we left" (see also Gavriel HaGadol, 1993: 123; Smallwood, 1991). In addition, many informants drew an analogy for me between this sojourn in Liberia and the Biblical Hebrews' wandering in Sinai before their return to Israel. Rakhamim explained, "We chose to stay there about three and a half years in order to get rid of the foolishness of America. To make a person born again. To die from the hell we came out of, to get rid of it—to learn, to get rid of the hate...to get rid of your bitterness.... Liberia was always conceived as the place where we would learn to be righteous. Those of us who wanted to do right shed off the hate and came home to Israel."

Well over half of the original 300 who made the trek to Liberia returned to the United States. Since today the Black Hebrew Israelite community is composed of more than 2,000 persons[14] most came directly from the United States without the benefit of a cooling-off period in Liberia. What drove them from their homes in American cities into the spartan, communal lifestyle of Dimona, Israel?

Below I shall present several individuals' autobiographical narratives to illustrate how they came to accept the meaning and message of the

Black Hebrew Israelite Community. The stories recounted to me focused on three often related themes: 1) the danger and evil of everyday life for Blacks in America; 2) the desire for a positive identity linked to a[n African] land, history and language, and 3) religious, spiritual, or mystical coincidences. Their confrontations with these issues shook the protagonists out of complacency and pushed them to consider an alternate knowledge base which they then used to reinterpret the past, challenge the present, embrace a radically new identity, and plan for the future within the Black Hebrew Israelite Community.

Several parents, in mulling over what inspired them to leave behind the lifestyle, the "piece of the pie," that they had worked hard to obtain—steady jobs, homes, cars, and plentiful wardrobes—mentioned their fears of escalating crime, and the desire to find a peaceful, gang-free, drug-free environment for their children. Even as they begin to discuss their lives in the United States, the elders, especially, shake their heads and say, like Rakhamim:

> America—what a nightmare! That was a nightmare to be in America. I was jumpy the whole time I was there. Every time a door slammed.... That's a horrible place! You walk on the street, everybody got a gun, all calling names, and they saying they gonna shoot somebody, and they mean that. You can't speak to nobody hardly. You speak to somebody and they say, "You know me?" What are you talking about? And you better not open your mouth. They just shoot you for nothing and just walk away. And nobody gonna lock them up. That's just the way they live. And who want to live like that?

Esriya, a registered nurse from Chicago, blending a matter of fact tone with a sense of higher-power coincidence, narrated a series of events that led her to follow her husband's lead and move the family from the U.S. to Israel:

> I came to visit (the Community in Israel) in 1979. I was impressed by the love people were showing for each other, and the peacefulness [but] I wasn't ready to move here yet... [Then there was all this] Black on Black crime, and things were hitting home. I was a public health nurse, as I had told you. I was making a visit [in Chicago], and I was trying to get in a house but I couldn't cause the door was locked. And as I was standing there I saw these 3 men knock down a woman, grab her bag—and another man was sitting in his car. He came out to me and asked, "Did you see these men?

They were watching you. And they were probably going to get you." Well, I was kind of shaken up….

Then another thing that had happened to me. I told you I had a white Lincoln. One evening I was stopped at a red light, and a young teenager came up along, took a crowbar and knocked in the window to get my purse—which wasn't on the seat beside me but down below between my legs. I called the police, but naturally nothing ever happened. Next day I had to take my car to get another window put in—sixty dollars from my pocket for that. I was beginning to think, This is getting too close to home.

Then another incident: someone was trying to burglarize our apartment! I lived in a three flat in the upstairs apartment and two aunts lived in the downstairs ones. My son was down at his aunt's, and probably left the door to our apartment open. The TV was out there on the landing, and a pillow case was gone with some jewelry. I called the police and they came and dusted for prints. My aunt had told me that the calculator was still on the table after the burglar had run, but when the police left, the calculator was gone! They took that calculator, but I never got any justice. That's the third incident.

The fourth: My son, he was a teenager at that time, when drugs and gangs came into the Black community. My son went to a dance, a social occasion, place to meet friends. As he's leaving a group of boys came over saying, "Buy this brown bag," forcing him to take it. My son related to me that he knew that it was drugs. He didn't want the drugs, he didn't want to give them money, and he said to himself, "I don't want to die." My son was saved by using his head, by lying down on the street, acting like he was having a fit, throwing his arms, mumbling and moaning, and foaming at the mouth. The other boys said, pardon the expression, "The nigger's crazy," and walked away leaving him alone. When he told us we were laughing so hard, but we were all scared too; he could have been shot dead.

This was the fourth incident in a period of about 2 years. I was thinking: There's got to be something better than this. And then on the news, all the time: children molested, drive-by shootings, gangs, violence.

By this time I was in my late 30s. My son was 17, my daughter 10, and I got pregnant. Never in my wildest dreams did I expect this, to be pregnant at 40. Abortion's not the way to go—I was a staunch

Catholic!—but I was struggling. In this day and age I didn't want to bring a child into this world. And then my husband asked if I wanted to go to Israel.

Esriya, and all the people I conversed with or interviewed about their decisions to come to Israel, concurred that the way of life they knew in America was not about to change for the better. They had theoretical knowledge and practical experience that crime, drugs, and materialism define the American urban experience, especially for Blacks. But unlike Esriya, whose husband was the initiator of their family's *aliya*,[15] most of the others focused their narratives not on fear of city streets, but on their search for identity and the answers provided by the Hebrews.

Yafa, Adiv, Yadiel, and Tumaya were upwardly mobile college students when, in the 1970s, they first made contact with the Black Hebrews. Yafa, in her succinct, no-nonsense style, told me that after one class she knew that she would be on her way to Israel:

> They just answered questions no one else would or could. Not just rhetoric but real answers about returning to God, to our roots....Once I was shown that in Deuteronomy it is explained if you sin and turn away from God you will be punished, I could understand why Black Americans were in this [terrible] position. I didn't want to be a nothing Black American, Afro-American, Negro American, and the Community answered my questions by providing an order, a solution, a righteous path to life.

At another meeting several weeks later she expanded on this theme:

> I had always been looking for an identity. An identity as a people, not just to be second-class, groping in the darkness. I was always asking these questions, challenging things when I was a kid, a teenager. I got to college—and I was tired. I wanted to do just like everyone else, follow the path. I went to this class just because of my sister. I was very much interested in what was being taught in the class.

*FM—Which was?*

> Basic history that connected African-Americans to the Holy Land. It was like a spiritual awakening. Things I had always felt but never heard. I could relate to this as truth. I thought, "This is it," and I was ready then to join the community. I was looking for an identity as

a people, not just to be second-class, groping in the darkness in a country that we didn't have a chance to make it in. I was very excited....For me, for each of us, it was a spiritual awakening.

Adiv, the vice-principal of the new school, came to Dimona in 1973 from Chicago. His explanation for how he found his way to the Black Hebrew Community begins not with a new revelation but with the "bits and pieces" of wisdom his parents had brought with them from the South:

My father was illiterate, but he used to always say little sayings, like "A small Black nation will rise out of the East to rule the world." I grew up listening to sayings like this, like Black people in America were direct descendants of the Israelites. Bits and pieces of things were said to me that created the spirit of the search for truth.

In college, years later, his Black roommate wore a Star of David, grew his beard and ate only vegetarian foods. Adiv asked him about these practices, and his roommate explained the connections between Black Americans, the Bible, and Israel. They were compelling.

Two years later he and me—9 of us, six brothers and three sisters— all came in '73. We dropped everything. We studied and kept our grades up while we were there, but then we put all our ideas of "getting over"[16] aside—they just died. Our goal was: come to Israel and serve the God of Israel.

While Yafa and Adiv were attracted to the Black Hebrew Community for similar reasons—it filled an intellectual, identificational, and spiritual void that participation in political movements and standard churches did not—Yafa's discovery about the Truth of her (and all Black Americans') origins in Israel represents a dramatic break with the knowledge of her past. Her parents did not take kindly to her decision and interpreted it a rejection of the life they had built, their understanding of how to get ahead, and their plans for her future. Adiv's narrative, by contrast, stresses continuity between his decision to join the Community and his father's remnant knowledge about Blacks' origins and destiny. Unlike Yafa, when Adiv told his parents he was leaving for Israel, his mother replied, "You would be the one."[17] Despite Yafa and Adiv's different backgrounds and the different reactions their families had to their declarations of being Hebrews, they both relate that their first meetings with Hebrews confirmed something that they had known all along in their hearts but were never before able to articulate—a subjugated, alternate knowledge of Black Americans' origins as Biblical Israelites.

Yadiel, also from the southside of Chicago, arrived in Israel in 1980. Since 1987 he has been in charge of the Community's organic farming project and is the Community's Minister of Agriculture. I had met him a few times in the course of my visits, but in early June we spent the better part of a day together. First I came to Dimona and then we drove about an hour together to the fields the Community leases from a moshav.[18] During the drive I asked Yadiel how he had found his way to discover that he was a Hebrew. "You must have asked this question hundreds of times." "No, about a dozen," I replied. "Then I am honored and blessed, and I will try to answer your question from two points of view: the historical point of view, and the personal. These both come together in my personal story." He began with the historical point of view, citing chapter and verse from Genesis to prove that the Garden of Eden had been in Africa, and from Deuteronomy and Leviticus in support of the prophecies for the double captivity of the Hebrews which he then connected to Africans' enslavement in America, "Now I'm not saying that all Black people in the US are Israelites or even that all of them will find their way back to this identity. What I am saying is that it is a fact, backed up by Biblical prophecy."

I interrupted Yadiel in the midst of his narrative. Something about it seemed too neat, too prepared, and, since Jews throughout the world carried the written as well as the oral tradition of their history (the Bible) with them, I wanted him to explain how the original Black Hebrews lost theirs. Yadiel side-stepped my question by emphasizing the oral traditions of Africa and Black Americans. He continued to give me a history lesson, emphasizing that, "Throughout all our history, in Africa, as slaves, and as Negroes, Black Americans, Afro-Americans, a handful of elders kept this identity alive through oral tradition," maintaining "Israelite camps" throughout the South and in the cities of the North.

I did not accept his clear-cut linear progression and asked him why these "Israelite camps" were such a small minority of the Black population. "Surely," I said, "the Baptist and other churches were much more popular among Blacks, both up north and in the south, and then later in the '60s, the Black Muslim movement took off. Hardly anyone in the US, Black or White, knows anything about Black Hebrews." Yadiel countered with the Biblical prophecy of captivity ending only when the Children of Israel live once again in righteousness. He continued to trace Black American history to support his points, concluding with the Civil Rights movement and the assassination of Martin Luther King. Finally, he posed the critical question of identity:

We can go through and see these different movements among Black people in America, their transformation from Africans to slaves, to Negroes, to Blacks, to African-Americans. Every people in America has an identity: Polish-Americans, Italian-Americans: they have a land, a language and a culture. What are Negroes? Blacks? African-Americans? Africa itself is composed of 50 nations, and within each of these, hundreds of ethnic groups with their land, language, and culture. African-Americans are the only group of Americans without an identity. It is only when we start to read the Bible as a record of our history that we can discover who we truly are. These Israelite camps kept it alive all these years, waiting for the moment. This is where my personal story joins the hermeneutic.

Yadiel then described for me how he grew up in Chicago, attending church every Sunday. But while that church filled his spiritual needs, it did not answer the question, "Who am I?"

I started asking this question when I was about 15, when Martin Luther King, Junior was killed. Why is it that every time a leader arises among the Blacks, he is shot down? We can't rise up on our own. And I started looking for answers. I was very attracted to the teachings of Martin Luther King, but I got more radical and militant after his assassination....

I had gotten radical, confrontational, and still I had no answers to that question, "Who am I?" I dropped out of society so I could find answers to that question. I spent my time reading; I dropped out of college for self-education. I read history, African history. Eventually I got my own apartment, I got a job: I worked down at the steel mill. I was moving out of being an American Black to looking at Africa, preparing myself with skills for going into a self-sufficient African community. I studied plumbing and electrician skills. I learned how to read architectural blueprints. A friend from High School introduced me to the, as we were calling them, Israelite camp. He took me to a meeting. And I didn't stop. By the end of the 1970s, I was on my way to Africa...and in 1978, I think it was, we went....And there in Africa I met with our community there. It was there I learned that our place as a people is not in West Africa, in Liberia or Nigeria, but in Northeast Africa, Israel. Following the prophecy, we returned to Israel the way we had come out. After three years in West Africa, I came on to Israel in 1981.

Yadiel's story, like Adiv's, stresses continuity but this continuity is not in the story of his specific family. Yadiel portrays himself at first as yet another groping Black soul, lost as a result of Biblical prophecy and the African diaspora.[19] Like Yafa and Adiv, he had felt an identity void since adolescence and strove to close it, but unlike them, he began with Africa.

With the publication of Alex Haley's *Roots*, and its serialization on television, thousands of Black Americans did the same thing. Bahtyah, by the beginning of the 1970s was a divorcee in her 30s, and a veteran of just about every Civil Rights, Black Power and Black Cultural organization. In Detroit, she moved from eye-opening discussions with Black Muslims to working in the Frederick Douglass Gun Club, to joining the Republic of New Africa; her autobiography stresses active involvement in forging a better future for American Blacks. In fact, she recalls that, "During this process my husband and I separated. He was deeply involved in materialism, and my commitment was to my people." But after a decade of this activity and some strong disappointments, she had decided to forego the struggle in America and move "back to Africa." She was ready to go in the summer of 1973 but at the suggestion of a friend, attended a meeting of the Black Hebrew Israelites, "I went to that meeting in July, and I left America for Israel in December."

Prior to studying with the Black Hebrews, Bahtyah revealed, "I had been impressed with the Bible as history, but ME? I didn't see any connection [between Blacks and Israel]. Israel? Isn't that the Middle East? Africa was our homeland. I was impressed with the Bible as [perhaps being] our history but I didn't see a connection. Until they told us about the Suez Canal. Prior to the building of the Suez Canal, Israel was landlocked with Africa. What it went along with is the way that Africa was carved up by European powers, partitioned during the Berlin conference. Between July and December 1973, everything I had been searching for came together. This tied all previous experiences together." Yadiel and Bahtyah, among others, began their search for origins quite logically in West Africa. The addition of the historical-spiritual element of the Bible, and further geographic proof that Israel had always been part of the African landmass, shifted their identificational focus from Liberia and Ghana in the West to Israel in Africa's Northeast.

Unlike any of the other 20 people I interviewed, Tumaya, who had spent most of her childhood in Louisiana, came from a family filled with Afrocentric culture. She did not move from a Black Baptist church or the array of civil rights organizations to the Black Hebrews. Tumaya grew up knowing who she was; she knew that she was the descendant of once proud African people who had been kidnapped and forcibly sent to America to be the slaves of White colonialists there. Her mother, who had been an adherent of Marcus Garvey in her youth, taught her children at home:

> all about our ancestry, and the different traditions, and rituals and things that our people practiced, the dress, the history of the great empires, and the kings, and all of those things, she taught us all of those things. And our surroundings looked like my surroundings look right now, she collected a lot of [African] arts and crafts....She had us dressing like this when we were young. I was in long clothing when I was young, into the different African hairstyles and things. I just grew up with that.

Despite her exposure and attachment to a rich cultural heritage, Tumaya relates that she was troubled about the contradictions she discovered in African history:

> It was during the time that I was at Howard [University], that I began to just feel that there was something else I didn't know about myself, about our people...some things didn't match, and some things didn't make sense. It didn't seem, it didn't make sense to me, that a people that was so great had gotten taken as slaves. It wasn't making sense to me. A lot of things weren't making sense to me.

> And then at Howard, I also decided to take a course that dealt with the Bible. And hearing in there about a people that was going to be enslaved and the things that happened to them, and how they turned their backs on God, and those kind of things, it also aroused something in me, but I couldn't make a connection anywhere.

Tumaya found this connection in the middle 1970s when her mother "discovered that Ben Ammi had gotten to Israel...so she wrote him a letter all the way here. And in response, someone from the community travelled to, she was living in Mississippi at the time, to see her. And she was very elated about all that she had found out. And she called me and told me and asked for me to come, you know, to hear it." In 1978 her mother and one younger sister joined the Community in Dimona; Tumaya, however, wanted to see more of the African continent first and went to Liberia— "we have a community there"—for a three year stint, which turned into six. Before settling in Israel, she felt compelled to see through the love and attachment she had always had for [West] Africa. Although she had come to the realization that Black Americans are the descendants of the Biblical

Hebrews and that their original roots were in Israel, it took some getting used to.

> So I spent those years there and then I came here. It was somewhat of a mind transition that I had to go through because I had grown up so much hearing that my connections only went as far back as the African, and not knowing that the African had a root in the Bible, that it was a whole mind transition that I had to go through in seeing myself as a Jew, as a Hebrew, as a, what did that mean? But the more that I heard and understood about our people, and how we came to be in the different slaveries that we were in, what was the reason for it, and how we were dispersed throughout Africa, and the building of the Suez Canal, and the separation of Africa from Israel, all of those different things began to make all of that clear for me. I just had to just transfer my mind (laughs).

> [At the end of six years] I was ready. I was ready to come. And it was like, as soon as my feet touched the soil here I felt something. I felt like I was home, and that I had finally made that final connection. I was where I was going to find out all I needed to know about myself, and all that I needed to do and be, and make all the changes I needed to make, and all the transitions, and everything. That feeling, it just came over me when my feet touched the soil here.

Beginning with the knowledge that her origins were in Africa, as well as strong cultural connections to the continent, Tumaya found her ultimate place in Israel-in-Africa. Like the others whose stories were presented above, working out the connection between the Bible, the peoples of West Africa, and the indignity of slavery, and then minority "no-identity" status in the United States, revealed to Tumaya an entirely different worldview from that based on the knowledge she had originally possessed. With this revelation came, concomitantly, an enhanced identity and inner sense of security. A dancer, musician and educator, she actively works to make manifest the connection between West Africa, where the ancestors of American Blacks lost their freedom, and Northeast Africa, their Biblical homeland, in her job as the director of the Community's Academy of Fine Arts. During the summer of 1994, Tumaya guided a group of young people from the Community on their first Cultural Heritage Trip to Ghana, to visit the slave camps from which their ancestors had been forcibly transported to America,[20] and to learn indigenous African crafts, dances, and melodies. Tumaya concluded her narrative by stressing the importance that the Israel-Africa links have for the next generation, especially for those who were born and spent their whole lives in Israel:

> The links they have to Africa—they have to understand that—and the link that Africa has to Israel—they have to understand that whole connection in order to really know who they are. Because that's the main thing that we lost in the whole chastisement we went through: we lost our identity, and we lost connection with our God, the God of Israel. So that's what we have to get back: our identity. We have to know who we are.

Documented history, as well as an oral tradition passed from one generation to the next, solidified in African-Americans the knowledge that they were the descendants of African slaves, who after the Civil War became second-class citizens under the weight of Jim Crow laws. Their identity then changed from a racial term, Negroes, to a political term, Black-Americans, and most lately to an ethnic label, African-Americans, as small groups gathered increasing strength to challenge racism and the laws that made it a social fact.

Despite changes in African-Americans' legal status and group identity, discrimination and minority status have as yet to disappear. This knowledge laid the groundwork for members of the Black Hebrew Israelite Community, while still young American men and women in Chicago, Detroit, New Orleans, to search for explanations for their, and their people's, tragic history. While thousands of Black Americans found these answers in long-standing European racism and the discriminatory legal code of the United States, and then addressed these problems by battling to bring about political change, Yafa, Adiv, Yadiel, Bahtyah, and others in the Community were unconvinced that "legislated equality" or "a piece of the pie" was the answer to Black America's plight. With the knowledge they had at their disposal, they looked outward and sought further than the United States and Europe for explanations and alternatives: they explored the implications of their acknowledged roots in Western Africa, and the messages of the Bible. In striving to counter the inadequate Negro-Black-African American identity foisted on them and its attached demeaning minority status, they became receptive to a different knowledge scheme that could provide an explanation for their people's noble but fallen history and, additionally, give to them and their people a sense of mission, a purpose in life.

In embracing the Black Hebrew Israelite Community, the discontent that stemmed from accepting the knowledge of the Eurogentile world, a knowledge they had had little choice but to espouse, was reversed. In forging a group based on the long-suppressed tie between West Africa and Israel, subjugated knowledge connected to the troublesome question of Black-American identity, came to the fore and became the doxa upon which a new, self-defined culture and community could flourish.

## Practical Action, Counter-Hegemony, and the Doxa of Righteousness

Pierre Bourdieu (1977) has shown how culture develops, becomes institutionalized, self-replicates and even changes as the result of practical action repeated over time. The Black Hebrews, proclaiming themselves, "a culture, a way of life," have built a community imbued with a sense of history, even timelessness, despite its mere 26 years of existence.

Each of the three times I took the official Community tour I was struck by the frequent usage of the word "tradition" to explain social patterns (such as "Divine Marriage") or items of material culture that were recently invented or accepted into the community. In describing the "Messianic suit," the Community's "signature garments"—a dashiki-like overblouse embroidered around the neck and on the sleeves, for the men, or a long fringed skirt for the women—Bat-El, the Community's head seamstress said:

> This is the suit that is to exemplify a tradition that will set us aside from any others, from Nigeria, from Ethiopia. You know an Ethiopian or a Nigerian from their clothes, we want to be known by ours. We've developed this concept that will set us aside….This is the garment used to represent the community.

I was told in more or less the same words about "ecos," or the cotton-crocheted, rubber soled shoes widely worn in the Community. Invented a matter of years ago as an alternative to store-bought leather shoes, Yafa, Shemaya, Tumaya and others described them to me as "part of our traditional dress."

Prince Rakhamim and I also had a lively discussion on the issue of tradition versus invention. He was telling me about the Community's early years in Liberia, how they set up rules and regulations for communal living in the camp. His description sounded to me like the group's leaders were creating rules on the spot, but when I asked him about it he defined this code of behavior as simply the implementation of Biblical injunctions to "do right." I kept pushing, but he maintained his stance:

*FM: So what you're saying is that at this point you decided to establish a new law, or reinvigorate an old law?*

Rakhamim: Re-invigorate an old law. And live it this time, not break it.

In reconnecting the legacy of the Bible with the heritage of Africa, both of which had been torn from them over centuries of dispersal and captivity, formerly Black American men and women found the "power to define" and built a community, a culture and traditions that have a tangible presence in Israel-as-Africa. Living out this connection through their communal lifestyle, Afrocentric dress, vegan diet, polygynous families, iconoclastic worship services and festivals, the Black Hebrew Israelite Community not only continues to convince its members that they are living out God's commandments to "do right" but also forces the issue of wider acceptance.

Every day, outside the boundaries of their *kfar*,[21] the Black Hebrews are confronted with another much more widely accepted and powerful knowledge system than their own, that of the State of Israel backed by Eurogentile interpretations of the Bible and World History. Indeed, according to Gramsci (1971:416,447), Western Culture possesses hegemony over the whole World Culture, and therefore its disapproval, denial and negation of the Black Hebrews' claims are just about absolute. The Black Hebrews, nonetheless, have rallied subjugated knowledge about Africa to counter Eurocentrism when they redrew the map of the world. But, at the same time, by underscoring the primacy of the Judeo-Christian tradition and corroborating its incontestable position of holiness and truth, they confirm the hegemony of European culture. Their placement of Israel in Africa, while debunking the geographic centrality of Europe in world history, does not contest the ideological base of its dominance. The hegemony of the Bible is so compelling that the Black Hebrews' way of challenging Eurogentile culture and its implicit racial hierarchy is not to reject the Holy Book, but to deny that the cradle of civilization that it represents was located in the Eurasian "Middle East." Instead, they shifted it to Africa, substituted Biblical figures' White faces with Black, and claim The Book as their own.[22]

This strategy serves to answer the critical question of (formerly) Black American men and women who grapple(d) with the question, "Who are we as a people?" and legitimizes their claims to the Great Tradition of the Bible. It serves too as a compelling rallying cry for the recruitment and maintenance of hundreds of people to conform to the Black Hebrew Israelite Community's strict rules for communal life. However, as they proclaim the Bible as the source of Truth, the Black Hebrews confirm too its essentialism, and thereby fail in the wider world, where everyone knows that the Bible is the story of the Jewish people, to expropriate it. Thus, professing the Bible to be their group history does not afford them much opportunity, especially in the Jewish State, to be granted "an alternative symbolic universe with an 'official' tradition whose taken-for-granted objectivity is equal to one's own" (Berger and Luckmann 1967:109). Indeed, if not ridicule, the Black Hebrews' claims arouse skepticism and suspicion on the part of Israelis whose territory, if not legacy, is under dispute from the Palestinians, who are tougher, more powerful rivals with a much stronger historical base to their demands.

The Black Hebrew Israelites are not the first African-Americans to identify with the Hebrews of the Old Testament (Adelfila, 1975; Baer and Singer, 1992; Brotz, 1964; Fishkoff, 1995; Hurston, 1984; Levine, 1977; Santamaria, 1987). They are, however, the first group to have rallied together the force of their beliefs to make an exodus out of America, resettle in Israel, and build a community there that in deed, as well as word, links Africa to Israel, Israel to Africa. In so doing, they have altered, if just a bit, a taken-for-granted world history that places Europe at the center and Africa in its shadow, giving to Black Americans the power, and a mission, to resurrect long-lost, subjugated knowledge and rebuild themselves as a proud people with a law, a language, a land, and an identity.

## Notes

1. Brochure entitled, "The Historical Connection of the Hebrew Israelite Community to the Holy Land," published by the Hebrew Israelite Community Public Relations Department.

2. Ben Ammi. 1990. *God, The Black Man, and Truth*. 2nd revised edition. Washington, D.C., Communicators Press, pp. 116–117.

3. The Black Hebrew Israelite Community defines the word divine as "that which is pleasing to God." Prior to the Ministry of Education of the State of Israel's provision of a standard curriculum for their children in 1993, the Black Hebrews taught them Divine Geography and Divine Mathematics, their interpretation of these subjects. By the same token, Divine Marriage is the term they use for polygyny, and Divine Agriculture their gloss for organic farming.

4. In the writings of Ben-Ammi, the Black Hebrew Israelites' spiritual leader, the term Eurogentiles is employed to refer to White Christian Euro-Americans. I shall use the same term in the remainder of the paper.

5. This is not to say that some members of the community have not dropped out over the years. They have. No one could or would provide me with exact num-

bers or statistics, but my hosts were eager to give me explanations. On a general basis I was told several times, "Our lifestyle is not for everyone. It demands dedication and sacrifice." On a more personal note, one of my hosts has a sister who lived for several years in the community but returned to America. Why? "Who can say exactly. We have very strong and strict rules in this community. No smoking. And sometimes people, they just want to smoke. Everybody has their weaknesses. I like sweets, and sometimes I just want to put too much sugar in my mouth. Not everyone can live by our rules. This community is not for everybody...." Another's mother returned to America. Some men left, searching (foolishly, my hosts added) for personal fulfillment; one wished to become a basketball player (at age 37!), another was lured by promises of riches. The Community acknowledges that people join and others leave and stress that all are free to come and go as they wish. What is most important for the leaders, spokespeople and members is that the Community not only maintains itself but grows every year; despite drop-outs it has been gaining in numbers, prestige and legitimacy in Israel and abroad, further evidence of its rectitude.

6. Primarily Chicago, Detroit, Atlanta, Washington, D.C.

7. This vegan-vegetarian diet eliminates the necessity of adhering to the Biblical code of kashrut since no meat, foul, fish, nor dairy products are ever served.

8. Black Hebrew Israelite women follow the Biblical laws of niddah which forbid sexual relations during the menstrual period and for a specific number of days after the birth of each child (40 for boys, 80 for girls). In addition, women are excused from performing normal household tasks during the time of their confinement, although they do not live outside their households.

9. A Community-specific holiday marking the return of the first group of Hebrews to Israel.

10. The Law of Return of the State of Israel stipulates that all Jews from throughout the world have the right to automatic Israeli citizenship upon return to Israel. The Law defines a Jew more broadly than the traditional matriline definition of halakha [religious law]; the Law of Return provides for individuals with at least one Jewish parent or grandparent. Since the Black Hebrews had none—most had been baptized in Christian churches—they did not qualify.

11. Here is neither the time nor place to recount the group's history, either from their point of view or from that of the Israeli government. See (Ben-Ammi 1990, 1991a, 1991b), Ben-Yehuda (1975), and Gavriel HaGadol (1993) for "inside" stories; Gerber (1977) and Singer (1979) for outsiders' reports. David Glass (1980) published a report [in Hebrew] of the State of Israel's decision regarding the non-immigrant status of the Black Hebrews.

12. On June 1, 1995, one of the Community's kohanim (priests), told me, as two school buses were loading up to take first and second graders for their "Discover-the Land" class trip:

We have much to learn about Israeli history and to learn from it. It is not our history; ours went in another direction. We are learning how to integrate into Israel. Discover the land - so much to know. We don't have full citizenship rights yet, but they are on the way. I keep telling the children: Get ready for the army.

You're gonna serve in the army. No, not in a combat unit, but in communications, maintenance, something. Get ready. We want to integrate into Israel but also maintain our own traditions and lifestyle because we have our own way of interpreting the Torah. We never want our children to smoke cigarettes and eat meat like Israeli Jews. And if the day comes when our children tell parents what to do, then we know we have failed in our job.

13. That is, Israel.

14. The Black Hebrews, citing the Bible, do not "count heads." I believe that in addition to this injunction, their imprecise numbers are a political tactic that blurs the true extent of their population and protects them from the threat of deportation.

15. Ascent, or immigration, specifically to Israel. This Hebrew word is used by the Black Hebrews in everyday conversation.

16. The expression used among Blacks for making it economically and socially. The term, "getting over" derives from the Biblical episode of the Israelites crossing, or getting over, the River Jordan. In "getting over," they left behind the 40 years of wandering in the wilderness that followed their exodus from slavery in Egypt, to begin life anew in a land of their own, the land of milk and honey promised them by God.

17. Subsequently, two and a half years later when he went home for a visit, four of his sisters accompanied him back to Dimona and joined the Community. Both his mother and his other sister have come to visit. His "brother was going to come, but he got a good job—AMTRAK—and couldn't or wouldn't leave. My father? He wouldn't get on a plane or a boat if his life depended on it!"

18. A moshav is a cooperative farming settlement in which each family has its own personal property and pools some of its resources to support capital equipment and large scale projects (i.e, greenhouses, orchards). It differs from the kibbutz which is a communal farm in which (until recently) all property belongs to and all income are contributed to the kibbutz's general fund. Redistribution of resources occurs on a by-need basis determined by the by-laws of the kibbutz.

19. Others, of course, might interpret his sense of alienation quite differently. Albert Memmi (1967:105) ponders the position of the colonized in the colonizer's schools, "The memory which is assigned him is certainly not that of his people...[for] He and his land are nonentities or only exist in reference...to what he is not...."

20. In our interview I could not help but draw an analogy with tours that the State of Israel arranges for teenagers to Poland in which they view the death camps of World War Two. Tumaya concurred with the parallel.

21. Kfar is the Hebrew word for village. The Black Hebrews apply this word, usually pronounced as two syllables, ki-far, in reference to the land and complex of apartments in Dimona that they lease from the Israeli government. This complex was built in the late 1950s to be an Absorption Center for Russian Jews who never came....

22. The Nation of Islam (Black Muslims) did indeed challenge the primacy of the Judeo-Christian tradition and embraces instead Islam, the third Great Reli-

gion of the Middle East, as the "true" tradition of the Black-African people. It is worthy of note that neither the Black Hebrews nor the Black Muslims have ever attempted to resurrect or redefine native belief systems of tribal Africa; one way or the other, they stuck with hegemonic cultures.

# Chapter 6

---

## Return to Womanhood: Construction of a Redefined Feminine Identity

### Hagit Peres

Why do the women in the Hebrew Israelite Community (HIC) choose to join a community which can be classified as a "New Religious Movement (NRM)?" By doing so they consciously choose to become part of the social controversy that often NRMs create within their surroundings. Simultaneously, they limit themselves to a "world of women," basically renouncing any prior aspiration for equal opportunities for both genders. The linkage between participation in social religious movements and redefinition of gender roles has been recorded by a number of observers (Aidala, 1985; Robbins and Bromely, 1992; Palmer, 1993; Rose, 1987). This chapter suggests that the reconstructed identity of HIC women is both a central attractive factor for recruitment of women and a benevolent or even therapeutic mechanism for creating new feminine self-esteem and empowerment. While the women in the HIC negotiate their status by constructing mechanisms for accommodation as a way of resistance within their patriarchal community, the insider voice of these women in the HIC is coherent with Bourguignon's (1980:334) conclusion that, despite the lifelong view of women as inferior to men, women may not have personal feelings of inadequacy or lack of self-esteem. Women in the HIC are proud of being women, mothers, and as they call themselves—"sisters in the sisterhood." Men, from their side, find occasions to show great appreciation for their "sisters" in order to secure their wives' cooperation in the fulfillment of their goals and aspirations. Both genders place great value on the domestic domain, which practically functions under women's supervision, although the final word over the households is that of the men. The particular structure of polygyny is a part of the organization of life in this patriarchy. Although long-standing conflicts between genders always exist, the achievement of stable and harmonious relationships between genders and inside each gender are major goals in this community. With its family-centered ideology, the HIC requires adherence to the traditional patriarchal division of labor and gender roles, but this traditionalist trend however is what attracts the women to the HIC.

## Introduction

It was sunset at the end of June, 1992 when I was invited for the first time to Dimona to attend the performance of "Sisterhood day." The festivities were just about to start with the traditional "evening prayer." As one of the very few guests in that year, I had the privilege of being the personal companion of Crowned Sister Yadah, then functioning as the liaison for the community for public relations. The spectacle of the prayer ritual almost paralyzed me when about two hundred sisters in long white dresses walked and danced in curving lines, softly singing, slowly approaching the central yard. There they formed horizontal lines in front of the central elevated stage. The light of the early summer sunset, covering the sky in reds and pinks, provided the perfect background for the scene. Traditionally dressed male priests conducted parts of the prayer. Sister Elisheva, an outstanding musician, accompanied the songs on an electronic piano. On the elevated stage sat the honorable leadership of the community: Ben Ammi, the Princes, and the Ministers, all of them men. A central part of the ceremony consists of a low bow by each sister in front of the "Father." This part is accompanied by a song constantly sung by the sisters, thanking the Father for his admirable work. At some point I joined the singing, and by so doing created around me reactions of astonishment. For a minute I thought I had made a mistake by singing, and asked if my singing caused any trouble? But Sister Yadah confirmed that, on the contrary, everybody was delighted to see me, an Israeli, enjoying their ceremony. I was overwhelmed, not only by the unfamiliar and spectacular festivity of women celebrating being women, but also by the fact that on this occasion I was one of the few Israelis to have witnessed this.

Geographically speaking, the community is located in the surrounding Israeli society, but by that time, very little relationship developed between both cultures and very little of the Israeli culture penetrated the invisible cultural boundaries of the HIC. Situated just a couple of miles from my own home town, and so close to my own culture, twenty or thirty years of isolation had created this "otherness" inside Israel, despite the Israeli government's efforts to extinguish this community.[1]

Once I could penetrate through the invisible cultural boundaries, I felt the impact of the unfamiliar way of identifying and of experiencing womanhood. The HIC's social isolation is interpreted here as central to the understanding of the social context of recruitment of members, in this case women to this NRM. In order to discuss the cultural construction of feminine identity in the HIC, there is a need to consider that women not only choose to join (and to contribute) to the formation of this traditional patriarchally oriented community, they also join a socially isolated community. By rejecting the western notions of gender and familial life, they not only challenge the immediate Israeli way of life, but also their former Western influenced African-American background. Therefore, the recruits find themselves socially isolated both from their prior social background and their present Israeli surroundings. This isolation, that so much characterizes NRMs (Beckford, 1985; Wilson, 1992; Barker, 1982), is an important factor in the construction of a distinctive identity. Given the linkage between gender identity and recruitment to a NRM, it is reasonable to look at the new alternative perception of gender within the HIC as a major attraction of this community. Moreover, the traditional patriarchal orientation is of particular interest in being defined as an attractive alternative for women in other places as well (Sherkat and Ellison, 1991; Wright, 1992). It is also of relevance to ask about the role of the African-American background in the establishment of the new Hebrew Israelite femininity.

By exploring the connection between gender identification and the attraction of women to a patriarchally oriented NRM, a challenge is presented to the widely discussed view that women's subjugation is necessarily a product derived from patriarchies as social structures. In the HIC, the explicit family-centered ideology in its patriarchal orientation indeed restricts women from many activities and in many ways, but it also provides women with gender related advantages. When women agree to restrict themselves to a traditionally defined female gender role (for example, by not assuming certain roles traditionally restricted to men or by placing public, formal, and political authority in the hands of men), women can gain freedom to create new areas for social activities. Even more important for them is that they regain a society based on the collaboration between both genders. Having men's support and appreciation is the center of the reconstruction of this feminine identity but the process of formation is not separate from inter and intra gender struggles. This chapter provides some insights concerning the process by which femininity is reconstructed.

## Joining a New Religious Movement: A Choice for a Change of Identity

Joining a NRM from the point of view of a private person is a serious process which involves various radical changes in a devotee's way of life. Beginning from the change of private name, status, occupation, and economic status, to the integration of new sets of beliefs, habits, and customs in the context of a new doctrine, all this and more create a sharp transformation of identity. Many of these transformations, as they are reported in sociological and anthropological studies are socially and personally positive processes in the sense that they channel new experiences into processes for healing the self and the society from the illness originated by society (Wallace, [1956]1979; Wallis, 1985; Straus, 1979; Anthony and Robbins, 1982; Palmer, 1993; Aidala, 1985). Even if they are positive, recruitment to NRMs involves serious personal sacrifice. Affiliation to NRM involves abandonment of prior social networks that later on will be replaced by a new set of social bonds (Stark and Bainbridge, 1980). Not less difficult in the case of the HIC is the abandonment of a geographical locus to move away thousands of kilometers to an uninviting country.

The personal stories that I constantly heard from HIC members were often related to their drastic decision to geographically abandon their prior American world. Such a drastic change in life must have some elaborated explicit rationalizations for this action. Another issue that very often arose in my conversations with members of the HIC was about the difficulty in dealing with the controversy that their new way of life creates for them both in their American and Israeli surroundings. My field notes contain many stories of bitter experiences connected with these decisions to change a way of life. Even in the present there is no defense against hard experiences with the surroundings. Often I hear about bitter or neglected daily contacts with Israelis. These conversations contain a wide variety of expressions. Sometimes there is a merciful understanding toward others' "ignorance." At other times plain frustration and irritation dominates

conversation about Israelis. The Hebrew Israelites may also express amuse-
ment or even an open derision of "the others." Life in a controversial group
that constantly challenges the western "eurogentilized" hegemony is a
source of great comfort and protection for those wounded from racial
segregation and social subjugation, while experiences with the surrounding society become a target for suspicion and rejection, it simultaneously
encourages seclusion.

Despite all the difficulties of living in the midst of social controversy,
the HIC has a strong explicit claim of belonging to "a righteous" way.
Living "a complete truth" in their divine society, they see themselves as
the only option for the creation of a perfect world. When I find a proper
opportunity I then ask my partner in a conversation to describe for me
his or her personal process of acquiring a new understanding of his/her
life and how these acquired new insights have led to drastic actions. "It is
a real transformation of the soul," one woman told me, describing the
deep-rooted changes. Recruitment, she believed, could promote great
changes in behavior, beliefs and even a transformation of personal tem-
perament.

What then stimulates the desire to participate in such drastic processes? Considering that sacrifices of many kinds can hinder the process
of affiliation with an NRM, it can be assumed that there must exist stimu-
lators that can overcome the hostility that the outside world transmits to
the recruits. In the case of the Hebrew Israelite women, feminine identification and gender roles are central attractions in the process of recruitment. First, for their abrogation of prior sexual confusion and ambigu-
ities, and second, for their ability to heal the wounds resulting from prior
sexual experiences.

## The Connection between NRMs and
## Redefinition of Gender Roles and Familial Structures

NRMs have flourished in the last few decades, especially since the second half of the twentieth century. This has demonstrated once again that
the formation and emergence of NRMs tend to increase in certain historical periods and becomes a phenomenon which requires consideration
of prior events as triggers for their emergence. Many sociologists and an-
thropologists of religion interpret this spiritual ferment as a response to
social strains (Wallace, 1956; Campbell, 1982; Anthony and Robbins, 1982;
Robbins and Bromely, 1992; Melton, 1993; Barkun, 1985; among others).

Cultural crisis, says Aidala (1985), appears as the fragmentation of cultural symbolic systems that had served before to integrate institutions and give meaning to personal experience. Robbins and Bromley (1992) note the significance membership and fellowship that becomes a home instead of an atmosphere that was not homelike before. They suggest that a gap forms between the highly institutionalized societies and rationalized public realms and the deinstitutionalized or under institutionalized private realm is what produces a disorienting environment to which NRMs respond.

While the emergence of the Hebrew Israelite's community in the mid sixties and early seventies, in the ghettos of the mid-west, was in response to racism and class stratification (Gavriel HaGadol, 1993), the factors which seem to have more influence at the personal level are emotional, social, and cognitive. Previous experiences of frustration, often associated with economic deprivation, loneliness, and inability to achieve central goals in life, as described before by Singer (1979, 1988:186), are common in the descriptions of the HIC members' backgrounds. The following narrative reveals in a characteristic way the influence of social strains in the African American society at the personal level. Moreover, it indicates the kind of action that followed in the specific case:

> At the age of 19 I lived in a poor neighborhood, my father was chronically unemployed and an alcohol addict and my mother worked as hard as she could to maintain the family. I saw for myself three possible futures: To marry within the neighborhood and inherit my mother's situation; to leave home, to go to college and then become a career woman who probably rejects part of her femininity; or to drastically change my life and affiliate to the Hebrew Israelite community and then gain my womanhood, a husband and a stable family within a substantial social order, and still be able to use my intellectual potentiality. The African American experience in the USA did not include the last choice alternative.

All the biographical stories, that vary in the description of their background details mention the dissatisfaction with their prior life and the attraction to familial life as dominant factors that lead them to the drastic decision to join the HIC. Aidala's (1985), Palmer's (1993), and Rose's (1987) reports include similar identifications: gender, sexual, and familial sets of values are central factors for attraction to NRMs. Citing Aidala's (1985:288) words on the matter: "We must consider age and sex/gender in our attempt to understand the impact of cultural crisis in the lives of individuals, and how this might lead to participation in religious groups.... Because gender roles are important links between culture and personality, as well as mechanisms for the allocation of social functions, rapid social changes and cultural fragmentation will be manifest as gender role confusion and uncertainty."

In an extensive research in ten different religious and secular movements in the USA, Aidala reports that despite the variety of conceptual alternatives offered by different movements, all communal groups were ideologically concerned about sexuality although their definitions of sexual/gender values differed greatly from each other. The range of approaches is divided by Aidala into three main categories: compulsory celibacy, group controlled marriages, and "free love." It is important to note that in all religious and quasi religious groups, sexual ideology is anchored by cosmic justifications which provide a set of rules to follow. Interestingly, Aidala claims that women, but not men, in religious movements tend to be more traditional in terms of personal gender orientations. Women who joined religious movements often rejected experimental approaches to sexual and gender activities or ideology (Aidala, 1985:310).

Palmer (1993) suggests a more complex categorization of sexual/gender approaches which are offered by social movements. She supports as well the claim that the experience of many women in the western world, especially around the time of their adolescence, is often painful and humiliating due to gender confusion, as well as to lack of clear perceptions of the culturally proper ways for action. These experiences lead women to reject sexual experimentation and to seek a more conservative alternative. Women, then, may be attracted to protective microsocieties where they can, as expressed in Palmer's words, "recapture a sense of innocence, and slowly recapitulate their stages of sexual/social development in a new cultural setting" (Palmer, 1993:52). According to this view, traditionalism can empower women in a particular way. It can provide them with the power to recreate what is for them a positive feminine experience. Rose (1987) looks at the familial social structure. According to her, a central benefit of conservative patriarchal societies is obtained from the fact that in these societies most families are constructed by women and men. Exclusive male roles provide men with prestige, magnitude and importance, now considered to be vital for the strength of the family. However, it is the patriarchal society which also requires the men to keep the burden and the responsibility of the family. Moreover, this reconstruction of relationships between genders usually does not stay within the limits of the strict traditional roles, of male as a provider and woman as a domestic organizer. Although based on this traditional dichotomy, new roles and expectations are built. For example, women can now use organizing skills for general social benefits, and men are expected to collaborate in educational roles within the domestic sphere. In referring to womanhood and femininity within patriarchal societies Rose writes (1987):

> Women rarely have completely or unconditionally accepted the patriarchal ideology of femininity that commands total submission of the wife to the husband. While women may be "successfully" socialized into behaving in "appropriate" ways that support the husband through sacrifice of the self, the behavior and attitudes of most women suggest neither total acceptance nor rejection, but rather accommodation and resistance to the traditional ideology of femininity.

The following paragraphs provide detailed descriptions of representative aspects of Hebrew Israelite women's construction of identity within the Hebrew Israelite patriarchy.

## Women Outnumber Men

It does not take long for an outsider who visits in the community's site in Dimona to notice that there are more women than men. Perhaps a conclusion that derives from a superficial estimation might be related to the fact that men are often at work, outside the domestic sphere, and therefore have less time to socialize with strangers, but many women work outside as well. A more careful survey, conducted as part of this research, reveals that the ratio between adult males and females is 1.67 women for each man. While this ratio does not show a great gap between males and females, it is interesting that the people from the community have estimated a much larger disequilibrium between female and male adults. The estimated ratios made by community members are 7:1, 5:1, 4:1. This difference between the survey and the community's own estimations underlines the insider tension between ratios of men and women. The relative high number of single or unmarried sisters may create strains by threatening married couples and entire families. Another aspect of this strain is the community's concern for the unmarried sisters and their desire to marry and fulfill their feminine role as women, wives, and mothers. These two factors are used by the community as arguments to explain how the custom of polygynous family became rooted in the community.

One can argue that it does not benefit women to outnumber men. However, one should note that since the community allows a man to marry more than one woman, single women are now allowed to pursue married men, while men are only allowed to pursue unmarried women. The way in that polygyny influences the status of women in the HIC will be discussed below.

Another explicit explanation for the tension resulting in the male to female ratio is the claim that women have a stronger tendency to affiliate with religious movements than men. Using the sisters' words: "women have been always closer to God than men." I interpret this phrase as an evidence of the HIC women's self esteem, as well as a reflection to the internal strength that women own as an entity by occupying a significant proportion of the community's population. Women's outstanding attraction to religion, is well recorded in the literature (Sherkat and Ellison, 1991; Haywood, 1983). Wright (1992) notes that the phenomenon of women outnumbering men is common for NRMs at certain phases of the communal development. Therefore, in summarizing the central argument, the unequal number of male and female members may expose women to weakness but also may be used to create strength. However, there is variation in the degree of culturally assigned desire and ambition to gain strength. These women do have a strong determination to gain self and other's esteem, and therefore they create the means to gain them.

## Adopting a Patriarchal Ideology Toward Gender and Family Structure

The biblical ethos, as it appears in Genesis, tells that after God created man in the Garden of Eden, he created woman from man. One of the Elevated Crowned Sisters, Atura Bahtyah Eshet Eliakeem wrote a book in which she interprets this biblical ethos and uses it to explain how and when the relationships between men, women, and God became lawful, and a model for what should be done.

> Woman was created to be part of man's flesh, blood from his blood, the feminine part of his God-mind, his essence or selfhood. ... The divine original meaning of women being created for woman was planned ... to be help, "fit" for man. To be suitable or appropriate for him. To adjust to his righteous lifestyle, to "fit" into his (God's) world (life). ... But things didn't go the way God meant they would, [and therefore] the world today is not the simplistic paradise of man's creation. Issues, choices and conditions have become complicated, complex and chaotic.
>
> (from: *Divine Marriage, Keys to Marital Happiness* by Bahtyah Eshet Eliakeem)

The text goes on to explain how man was tempted by women to go apart from God's way, causing the devastation and deterioration in the world as it is until today. The lesson that should be learned is that the "original" and "natural" Divine order of the different entities that construct this world (God, Man, Women, and children) must be accepted. The reasons for such order must be internalized and accepted by each entity, then the establishment of a solid basis for self-acceptance and mutual relationships between each entity and the others will be accomplished.

Aturah Bahtyah's text has a clear explicit message for the sisters: know who you are and behave properly according to our defined social standards. One can claim that she commands women to restrict their activity to the traditional domestic domain and leave the political and formal domain to men. The Divine order expresses publicly that women's status should be located under the men. Men have clear dominance over the political and formal domain. Nevertheless, as many studies on gender have shown, by creating a strong separation between the two gender spheres, each sphere gains internal strength as well as growing interdependence between the spheres (Bourguignon, 1980:334; Lamphere, 1974; Abu-Lughod, 1990). This provides women with ability to extract power and identification from the domestic domain.

It required a strong separation from the so-called "western" world to view housework and childcare tasks as a vital part of women's activities. Although HIC women may protest about the exhausting nature of housework, no feelings of unhappiness because of housework are expressed. Some women even gained their status as female leaders within the community for being outstanding examples of house management. By defining women as "the feminine part of God's creation" women are committed to provide their best talents, skills, and abilities for acting primarily in the domestic domain. Beside domestic power, women also have, to borrow Bourdieu's (1977) sense of the term, practical or unformal domain over politics and social spheres and processes by being organizers and responsible for central public activities. Some degree of the political domain is also formally in the hands of women: the sisterhood as an entity is authorized to make and to influence certain decisions that take place in public gatherings. This is done by opening subjects to discussion and a democratic vote. In other cases women may be in charge and hold authority over men as well. In these cases the validity of a role is measured by its productivity or by its social importance. These are the cases where the conscious will to divide domains into two separate gender spheres disappears. Certainly, women can and do contribute by using their creativity, skills, and talents in various fields; many of them working together with men.

However, women are instructed not to compete with men. Aturah Bahtyah's text has an explicit warning to women against threatening men: "Woman imposed her self-will into the sphere of Divine Authority and influenced man, who had received his instructions directly from God, to do likewise." The biblical woman and man and the "nature" of their relationships are metaphorical for all women and men. Here there is an aspect in which women can be dangerous for their society with their power to seduce men. Men from the other side, can easily lose control over their life by being seduced to disobey God. According to Murphy and Murphy (1974) women's threatening attributes appear in various cultural ethos and legends. The function of these stories is to warn men from letting women destroy the "proper" social order. Usually these stories are related by men as part of their masculine conception of the social order: men are warned not to give too much power into the hands of women. It is important to note that the ethos described above is related by a woman and for women. The lesson is that women must not "impose" their power (or self-will) to influence certain things in the society. I suggest that the very fact that women are the tellers of this patriarchally oriented ethos, implicitly demonstrates the almost invisible power of women. Through the telling of this biblical story, one can recognize a power that must not be publicly shown and admitted, but yet, silently recognized. Once it is recognized, then women gain a kind of esteem for acquiring power, but then they also must assume the responsibility not to misuse this power to destroy the society.

To summarize this part, two major interpretations on women's empowerment within the society were presented. Both are related to each other. Although they may sound contradictory, they are mutually displayed in daily life without producing major conflicts. The first is a structural hierarchical ideology, which places men in a clear public and formal superiority in respect to women, although practically in daily life, a higher degree of symmetry exists between both genders. The recognition of women's power in the practical realm is important for this is where women can best accomplish their desires for personal development and fulfillment without clashing with the patriarchal structure. The second is not loudly pronounced but it assumes that women have a lot of power. This power can be sometimes negative and destructive and therefore it is irresponsible to use it or even express pride of it. But then, the unadmitted knowledge about its existence along with the developed ability to control negative power can be in itself empowering.

## Polygyny from a Women's Point of View

In the Hebrew Israelite Community approximately 37 per cent of the marriages are polygynous (from a sample of 114 marriages reported during a survey in 1992 by this author). The existence of polygyny locates the community's ideology toward the family as both conservative and experimental. It is true that polygyny appears in the Bible, but not as an obvious family structure. Neither is polygyny (at least in its formal way) common in western society, nor even among family-centered NRMs. However, it is true that for the African-American members of the community, the custom of polygyny is connected to their African roots. We can also take into account McDaniel's (1990) claim that there is a continuity between African cultures and African family structures and those of African-Americans that were used to resist the difficult circumstances which were created in the Diaspora after slavery. McDaniel points that although the African family structure changes from place to place, the common cultural concept does not concentrate on the nuclear or conjugal family but on the extended kin group. Therefore, polygynous, matrifocal and extended families or kin and semi-kin groups are to be accepted as traditional African-American familial structures preserved from an African heritage (see also Monogan's 1985 rethinking of matrifocality). While polygyny per se, is not a part of the legitimate set of values in the African-American culture, matrifocality does appear frequently (Stack, 1974).

Since matrifocal families depend on the cooperation between women in the formation of households, it is then tempting to accept McDaniel's (1990) as well as Monogan's (1985) theories which view continuity between original pre-slavery African cultures and the African-American culture. However, despite the rationalized connection to the past, some of the senses of polygyny appear in the eyes of the community as an innovation, a new structure that required constant elaboration and maturation until its present formation. The introduction of polygyny was not instantaneously accepted by the women as a legitimate custom. It took almost three decades to develop polygynous marriages into their present form and to gain the experience needed in order to maintain such marriages. Coming from "Western" conceptions, one can guess why women (at least those who were already married) did not show much enthusiasm toward polygyny. But despite the protests of women against polygyny, it is the existence of it today (and in such ratios) that tells about the resistance and accommodation of the women of the HIC.

The following narrative was given to me by a most admirable woman who is also an Elevated Sister and was an informal leader since the beginning of the community in 1963. I'll call her "Mother Sara." This most beautiful narrative tells about her hard days facing polygyny for the first time, when the laws of polygyny were not yet formally established within the community. It is important to note that this very woman who suffered so much from her private experience in polygynous marriage, still was a vital source of inspiration and example of righteous feminine behavior for other women.

> In 1967, I got to Liberia with three children and pregnant.... [Here she describes the hard conditions of the foreign country: living in tents unsuitable for the heavy Monsoon rains, the difficulties in adaptation to the local food which only increased her pregnancy nausea and consequently weakened her] ... My husband came to Liberia two months later and he didn't say nothing about his [recent] second marriage. I found it from letters he had left in the tent from his other wife. I was so offended and disheartened. I didn't want to hear any explanation. After a while, his second wife came to Liberia, and she tried to establish some kind of relationship with me, but I rejected her ... what saved me was to concentrate in my work: work, work and more work. I tried to ignore my marriage, not to think about it.... At this time I thought it wasn't right to marry more than one wife. I couldn't understand why Abba [the leader] was so right in everything but in allowing multiple marriages he was not. Externally, I continued to show endless faith. But deep inside I wasn't really convinced with his righteousness. I prayed with all my heart to get the understanding, until I finally came to accept and fully understand what Divine marriage is about.

After more than 26 years in her own polygynal marriage Mother Sara can tell that there are advantages in the structure of the polygynous family. Mother Sara had participated since the early times very actively in the elaboration of "proper" preparations in marrying families for the acceptance of new brides. As a Crowned sister, Mother Sara has counseled many families when having problems in their marriages. Probably some of her tasks have also been involved in advisement for cancellation of requests for marriage (formally submitted to the HIC authority of the priesthood) where the participants did not convince the authorities to be substantively competent as partners for marriage. Talking about the acceptance of a co-wife the experienced counselor Mother Sara explains:

> Any woman who is involved in the process of polygynal marriage of her husband with another wife, goes through a crisis which she

has to overcome with the help and the sympathy of the other parties, especially that of the new bride. The case is much easier today,
when polygyny is not something uncommon anymore and there
are many who can provide advice from their own experiences. One
thing that I've learned is that while in this type of crisis, a married
woman has to stay close to her husband. Opening one more conflict with him, will put her in a more difficult situation.

One can suppose that by involving more than two adult participants
in marriage, polygyny is a structure that is likely to invite conflicts. Therefore, in order to make such a marriage viable, women's collaboration is
essential. After all, co-wives in the HIC reside in the same house often
sharing one room between them. Being so close, each of the "sister wives"
may spend more time together than with their shared husband.

The experience described above, displays the essence of strategies of
resistance and accommodation. Overt resistance is not meant here, but
the development of internal strength to resist devaluation by the means
of accommodation. Anyon (1983:21–23) clarifies the dialectic relationship between resistance and accommodation and how thin is the bound-
ary and complex the relationship between both actions. Accommodation
and resistance are two combined forms for a single process in which one
accepts what should not be avoided and simultaneously fights individu-
ally and as a group to save one's selfhood.

Not without internal struggles, Mother Sara continued to work and
contribute to the community and at the same time she prayed to God "to
give her the right understanding" in order to deal with the unavoidable
situation. If the women's strategy instead would have been to forbid their
husbands' marriages to more wives, probably this community could not
survive. However, Mother Sara along with other sisters were convinced
that the only way to salvation from their prior American life was in this
creation of a family-oriented new life. Therefore, they strategized to ac-
commodate in acts of resistance and to resist by strengthening themselves
within the structure of the patriarchy. Eventually the women even learned
to appreciate the benefits that could be extracted from polygygnous marriage.

Today it is not rare to hear declarations from women that are consci-
entiously willing to introduce another wife into their families. Even men
declared in front of me that they consider marrying another women because of their concern for their wives, who are engaged in too many social
responsibilities. These men said to me they were not searching for new
adventures of any kind that interested them, but the care for someone else

to help their wives in the house. Of course, men do enjoy the possibility of an additional love affair, without the need of breaking their prior family. However, good relationships between co-wives are considered essential to the establishment of polygynous matrimony. This is why some husbands send their first wife to make contact with a possible candidate before starting any new relationship. If the two women do get along well, then the field is open to start new relationships.

Strategies of women toward polygyny are diverse. Of course, not all marriages are successful, but the record proves that it can work. As we go into details, we would notice that strategies are mainly designed by the personalities acting in each case. The intention here is rather to provide a key insight that covers most strategies rather than to go into details describing the many reactions toward conflicts which can develop. This key is of course the decision of these women to live in harmony with their womanhood, with and within their society, rather than to provoke open conflicts around themselves. This approach to life had to be rationally internalized. It was a real innovation that came with the abandonment of the prior mode of thinking and feeling.

## Summary

The purpose of this chapter has been to understand an "other" conception of womanhood and femininity. This other conception is a constructed innovative understanding on the part of women that comes from the decision to abandon one cultural setting for the construction of a substitution that is believed to be better. The description of this conscious process of changing identities and rational approaches toward the social reality by women, exposes the reader to the complexity of human reaction toward conflicting and subjugating situations.

This description of the general ameliorating relationships between genders that comes along with the acceptance of a patriarchally defined social order, may sound too good to be true. In fact, whatever it is, it does not take into account the failures of the system but only the successes. Certainly, the structure and ideology of the HIC's patriarchy did not succeed with every one. It would be Palmer's (1993) suggestion that most members of NRMs stay only temporarily and only few persevered in the hard core for a lifetime. This could serve to lead to further investigation in order to discover if the NRM played any therapeutic role for those who stayed in the HIC for only a short time and then left. Another aspect worth exploration is the situation of HIC women who belong to the second generation, in their mediation between the traditional HIC feminine identity as it was transmitted to them by their parents and what they accept from the media and the world surrounding them in times when the community opens to the wider society.

However, here the focus was on the first generation of sisters who chose to join and succeeded to adapt to (and in) this patriarchally oriented doctrine and way of life. Lessons that these sisters have learned, from prior life experiences in the world, brought them to seek for a protecting family centered society. Although joining the community was a conscious choice, women had to confront newly created obstacles of "bringing the men back home" and giving them power to rule over it. It is in the search of alternative means to approach power that these women have succeeded. Strategies of accommodation and resistance facilitated their physical and spiritual belonging. The HIC women reaffirmed the traditional ideology of femininity and inequality between genders by proclaiming that the "women's liberation movement would not save them from the chaotic devastation now existent in the world." They rather decided to transform a patriarchal system into a livable atmosphere where the major advantage is a family structure with collaboration between genders and minimization of competition that can achieve better harmony.

The redefinition of selfhood was benevolent for these women, although it defined femininity in restricted terms. As shown above, the sophistication of any interpretation can make a big difference in life. The HIC women's view is that women's liberation has gained another sense of liberation: the liberation from the binding expectations of the western society, where they were unhappy.

## Note

1. In recent years, more than twenty years after the HIC was (unformally) established in Israel, social boundaries between the HIC and its surrounding Israelis are gradually decreasing. Contacts with Israelis are now much more frequent in many fields of life. Now Israelis teach in the school of the Hebrew Israelite children, and Israeli guests in the community have become a very common event.

# Chapter 7

## The Community as Mediator

### A. Paul Hare

Over the years the leaders of the Hebrew Israelite Community made public announcements about their willingness to mediate between African-Americans and the Jewish Community in the United States and in other areas. Although some of their members, such as Prince Asiel, to be quoted here, are based in the States, most of the community members live in Israel. Thus, Ben Ammi, who had previously renounced his American citizenship, was only able to return to the US to take part in mediation after his citizenship was reinstated.

### Mediation by Private Individuals

Bercovitch and Rubin (1992) have edited a series of accounts of mediation in international relations by mediators who range from private individuals, through regional organizations and the United Nations, to the super powers. Although the mediation by leaders of the Israelite Community does not fall in the international category, it has the characteristics of informal mediation by private individuals (Hare, 1992). In Rubin's (1981:7–19) terms, private mediators often seek an invitation to mediate but also can be invited, are conflict-managing, advisory (since the individuals have no formal authority to direct), and temporary. They are also relationship-facilitating, impartial, informal, and often individual, although a team can be involved. A characteristic of the formal mediator that the private individual does not possess is the power of economic or political backing.

Mediation involves attitude change and as such all the literature on attitude change applies (McGuire, 1985). However in this case one individual is not trying to change the attitude of another, but is faced with two individuals (or groups, or organizations) who may need to change their attitudes about each other before the mediation process can begin and will probably need to change their ideas about a solution to their problem if the solution is to have a lasting effect. There are four basic ways to change attitudes and influence a person to conform to a new idea: by offering or denying facts or material reward, by offering power or using coercion, by offering or denying friendship, and by calling up common values or denying the importance of others values (Hare, 1993a:63–72). Offering or denying rewards is only effective in the short run, until a new issue arises and a reward must again be offered or denied. Persuasion based on values, which become internalized, is the most effective because it does not need continual reinforcement.

Ideally a mediator is in a position to understand the point of view of both sides of a conflict and help the persons in conflict discover a new, overarching, idea concerning their interrelations by which both sides can experience some gain without detracting from the other. As we shall see, the experience of the Black Hebrews, as African-Americans living in Israel, provides them with an understanding of both the African-American and Jewish Communities in the United States. Their commitment to a righteous life provides a set of overarching principles that makes it possible for them to suggest activities that will reduce the conflicts between peoples, people and nature, and people and the righteous life. Sister Yadah notes the importance of having a community, as a model, where the principles of conflict resolution can be applied. In the case of the conflict between African-American gangs in Chicago, we will see that Prince Asiel was able to reduce the overt behavioral violence, only to discover a larger problem of more "structural violence" concerning a network of drug trafficking that lay below. Although as Ben Ammi mediates between people and nature and people and the righteous life, there are precedents recorded in the Bible that can still be applied as "absolutes." However the mediator still has to help formulate creative solutions since some sources of conflict, such as AIDS or the dumping of toxic wastes, were not prevalent in earlier times.

# An Interview with Sister Yadah (December 1994)

*Question: Describe your experience talking to a group of visiting African-American leaders in Jerusalem.*

A vital role for Israel that we see ourselves able to play is to mediate between Israel and African-Americans and also between the Jewish community in America and African-Americans. Over the years one of the major goals of the American Jewish community was to resolve the conflict that existed between the two communities there. We are a vehicle to accomplish that goal for the American Jewish community and for Israel as well. We have come out of the African-American experience and now have lived in Israel for 25 years. We have seen both sides of the coin. We look for ways to make the two communities one, or at least reach a point that each community has an understanding of the other. Having come out of the American experience of racism and second class citizenship, we have now in Israel developed a relationship with people whose skin color is lighter than ours. We find in Israel brothers and sisters of different colors who have come out of the same heritage. If we have a common heritage, we must have a common goal. We wish to help others understand what this means.

When we were called upon to go to Jerusalem to speak to a visiting group of African-Americans, we found that their experience in America was still that of hostility. We had to convince them that the experience we had in Israel indicated that there was no ceiling that would keep you down, but only the problem of finding the ladder that would let you climb the wall. Here the obstacle was more religious than racial.

On several occasions young Jewish students have visited our community. One group of teenagers from Britain had come to Israel to become familiar with their heritage. The organizers of the program want to give them a sense of being Jewish. I found myself asking them questions about their vision for life and their role and responsibility to show this light to other nations and other peoples. They had not thought about it because their heritage had not been presented to them in this way. So we were mediating between them and their Jewish heritage. They were living in conflict without realizing it, since they were just living out their lives like everyone else. There was conflict between who they were and their real purpose for being here. They had been taught to maintain tradition without any real responsibility for fulfilling the vision from their past.

*Question: What were you asked to do when you went to Jerusalem to speak to the group.*

The American Jewish Congress is one of the major American Jewish organizations with representatives in Israel. One of their ongoing tasks is to convince people that Israel is not as bad as it seems from articles in the press or reports on TV. For all of the conflicts that are seen on the six o'clock news, it is not that bad, it only looks bad. They bring to Israel persons who have been targeted as rising leadership in the African-American community, for example, someone who might become a congressman within the next five or ten years or a strong civic or social leader. They want to give them a positive bird's eye view of Israel by exposing them to various groups in Israel such as the Palestinians.

They invited us to make a presentation on our community, to give first hand information on our experience in Israel. First I gave a general overview of the community. Then I summarized the years of conflicts we have had with the Israeli government. Then I showed that we have turned to a new page and that political problems are not what they were, that progress has been slow but sure. Some of the persons in the group did not readily accept this. They asked: "Why has it taken 20 years to solve the problem?" Others wanted to know if the problem was racism. It was not very easy to explain to fellow African-Americans, out of whose experience we came, that we see the conflict as more religious. They see the conflict as racial. It was a very interesting experience.

We never spelled it out as being mediators or resolvers of conflicts, but the only way to get away from the idea that the problem is racism is to broaden your perspective. This is how we see our role. We find that the American experience for many, especially African-Americans, can be very limited.

*Question: Can you think of any other occasions?*

We entertained an Israeli group from the Nature Preservation Society. One guide has been bringing groups over a period of two years. He said: "We call ourselves the organization for the preservation of nature, but we do not actually practice it. So if there is anyone who is really doing this, it is the Community because you have incorporated this into your life style." Members of the Community are mediators between nature and people seeking to find a closer link with nature, to show how this can be accomplished in your day to day life.

When we use the word "mediator" my mind keeps going back to the life of Moses and Noah, they were mediators. Usually when people think of a mediator, Moses and Noah do not automatically come to mind. Yet a mediator is someone who has a perspective of what is best and tries to bring people into that understanding so that they will function in a realm that will cause positive results for them. This was the role that Moses and Noah played on a greater scale. Noah perceived that God was displeased and knew what His intentions were. Noah said I have to build a safe house, an ark.

As mediators, members of the community are perceiving God's displeasure through the events of the day and the circumstances surrounding us. We see that his displeasure will cause a great deal of wrath to fall upon mankind. So it is time to seek a refuge, not just for our selves, but to convince others to take that refuge. The Community provides an example of peaceful coexistence which can be taken anywhere and adapted to the local conditions.

## An Interview with Prince Asiel (September 1994)

*Question: How did you become involved with conflict resolution between African-American gangs in the US, what did you do, and what will happen in the future? In what respects was your participation in the Community a part of this?*

In Chicago in October 1992 Dantrell Davis was walking to school with his mother when he was murdered. This was on the North side of Chicago in an area called Cabrini Green, which was the center of the community leadership more than ten years ago. It was that incident that was so horrible, that a young life was snuffed out for no apparent reason. This aroused the sensibilities not only of the city, but of African-American men to a point where they could no longer sit on the sidelines. Several of the women's organizations in the Cabrini-Green area, specifically a group call "Tranquillity, Peace" which is headed by Marion Stamps, a civil rights activist who had marched with Dr. King, spoke to me and to other African-American men in the community and said "When will Black men stand up and challenge this assiduous system of destruction of young African-American lives?" I have a television program in Chicago called "A Spiritual Alternative" which I do once a week. On that TV program Marion Stamps made that plea. She said that they would have a demonstration the following week to recognize the death of Dantrell Davis and celebrate his life.

I was planning to leave the country. I put it off for a day because I was asked to join the demonstration. Prior to the demonstration I went into a community center where there were approximately 30 young African-American males. Some were in their late thirties and early forties. They said that they represented various street organizations, that are usually designated as gangs, such as the Vicelords. One of the leaders read a five page statement acknowledging their role in destabilizing the community for the last ten years. Both through misunderstanding and disinformation. The problem was how to get over it in the ghettos of America. They were prepared to talk and turn around if the community would receive them.

I was moved by the statement. I took the point and said if you are prepared to negotiate and to sit at the table, I will be part of that negotiation and bring in the community to have a dialogue and listen. So on the 26th of October a press conference was called in Chicago, the headline of the papers said "We will stop the killing." I took on the challenge to stop the destruction of men, women, and children. I did not take it on to stop drugs. I did not take it on to stop violence between drug dealers. I wanted to see if the community could be made a safe place where the elders would be respected, the children respected, and women would not be violated.

Based on that, I then took on the task of going to the community. I went to the religious community first. I felt that this was a moral issue that needed the support of the religious community, its vision and leadership. I then went to the African-American political community, the councilmen and the State representatives, to solicit their support so that I would not be misunderstood for representing gang leaders who were criminals. There must also be some economic program. If they were to turn their lives around there must be some alternative. The danger was two fold: first would the gang leaders be trusted or would this be a smoke screen so that they could expand their nefarious operations; second, would the community understand my role as an instrument to give the gangs credibility and visibility?

Then I began negotiations in what I thought were neutral grounds, "People United to Save Humanity", this is Jessie Jackson's organization. We went not only to the civil rights organizations but also into the churches. The churches provided a background where no one would be violated because we always had to meet on neutral ground. Before these men would not participate because they thought that they would be set up and killed. We created an environment in which it was at least possible to have a dialogue. Once that was achieved, I knew I had to go to the prisons. The prisons are like a hotbed where these men are being groomed for gangster activities. I went to the heads of groups such as The Black Disciples, the street organizations. Those who were recognized as leaders. If it was going to work these are the men who would have to say to their street lieutenants, "Stop." I asked them if I could use their names, they said yes.

An organization was formed among the gangs called "United in Peace." A button was designed with the twelve symbols of the various street organizations. So "United in Peace" became the vehicle though which the various organizations would come together and discuss turf, conflict, in terms of one member being in a neighborhood that he was not supposed to be in. They began to talk. "How did all this get started? Why do you want to kill him, for wearing his hat to the left or to the right?"

"How did all this get started, when you are 17, 18, or 19 years old?" They said: "The older brothers passed this on to us. We don't know why. It was so tragic because we have inherited death, we do not even know how to make peace. No one has ever taught us how to make peace." I realized how sad it was because the role models that could bring an end to the conflict had moved out of the community. I formed a mentoring program. So that the community could not be mislead, I went to the African-American Police League so that the community could see that there were those who were about law and justice, not just law and order, as code words. We had African-American policemen who had the respect of these men. For years they had demonstrated their authority.

We then began to organize the community. The community called a planning conference in Jamaica, on Montego Bay. Why did we go all the way to Jamaica to have a conference? For two reasons. One was that it was the home of Marcus Garvey who was one of the foremost nationalists and I thought that the spirit of it would be beneficial. It was a neutral environment where you could feel that political forces could not influence proceedings. They could speak their minds freely. There would be no radio and television. We spent five days down there and came out with some sound resolutions. Then we had to translate the resolutions into organizational work.

Historically individuals who had been doing the work felt that they were not recognized. We found that we were dealing with egos. We had to go and call as many people as we could who had been working with drug rehabilitation and with various organizations. I was then approached by several organizations to join their organization to be a spokesperson. I was asked to co-chair a committee for a campaign called "Black on Black Love." I agreed. An advertising agency was placed at my disposal that created billboards throughout the city saying "Imagine, no more violence," with the symbol of the twelve Nations, looking to the horizon to the future. Then a conference was called by Carl Upchurch after the Rodney King rebellion. He would try to bring the gangs together. There was a national gang summit in Kansas City. It brought over 300 participants from 21 states and 64 cities, including Hispanic and African-American women as well as progressive Whites. At that three-day conference in Kansas City people came together and fashioned a five-point agenda that was presented to the American Justice Department in terms of the brutality cases and economic parity to develop 500,000 jobs for inner-city youth.

From that we launched a program to go from city to city. We left Kansas City and went to Cleveland, Minneapolis, and Chicago. The Chicago summit ended a year after we started. At the Chicago summit we were able to bring Jessie Jackson, Rahbee Ben-Ammi, of the

Hebrew Israelite Community, Dr. Ben Chavis, Louis Farrakhan, and representatives of the Congressional Black caucus. So that the community could see that there were African-American men who had chosen to be in the forefront of the community.

One of the things that we did not anticipate was that crime was big business in America. There were forces who did not want peace to come. A business magazine reported that crime in America is a 473 billion dollar a year business. The drug business in Chicago and the suburban area is 7 and a half billion dollars a year. In the State of Illinois the budget for prisons is 856 million dollars a year. Sixty eight per cent of the prison population in the state of Illinois is comprised of African-American males. However, only five per cent of the State's population consists of African-American males. We saw that crime was big business. In our naivete there were those who said that there could be no peace, that it was all a hoax, all a farce. We did not realize that we had disrupted drugs in these communities. That if peace would come it would no longer be profitable for these men to be on these corners any more. So criminals began to bring guns back into the community. They armed new youngsters who would work for two or three thousand dollars a day selling drugs, to take over these corners. We saw that the peace that we had would not last. We had not understood the depth of the problem, we could put a fire out and another fire would start.

By the end of the year we chose three areas in Chicago to prove that it could work: Altgeld-Gardens, Cabrini-Green and Englewood. Englewood was the murder capital of America. One hundred homicides had taken place in that 5.2 square miles. We reduced the number in one year to five homicides. In Cabrini-Green there were no gang related murders in one year. In Altgeld-Gardens we reduced crime by 50 to 60 percent. Over all crime in Chicago after six months had dropped by twenty three per cent. The problem became exacerbated because of political opposition. Politicians felt we were now organizing gang members as political parties. We organized a program called "21st century vote." We placed 35 to 40 thousand new people on the roles, which helped elect the first African-American female senator for the State of Illinois. Secondly, they were able to organize themselves and challenge the political system. When the schools were closed we were able to put 12,000 people on the street marching around city hall to demand that the schools stay open. The political opposition was great. They began to malign my name. They scared social activists as well as political activists away from the movement. We felt that one has to deal with drugs at the consumption level. We could not do anything about pushers or distribution because that was a worldwide network. We realized that if we could change people's lifestyles and appetites we could affect drug consumption, and we did. At the end of the year we found we had many successes. We went to Washington, D.C. to hold a conference to plan the next two to five years.

I have been committed to conflict resolution in the streets of Chicago and across America for the past year. I have been in almost 10 cities in the last year. I am scheduled to go to Washington, D.C. in the middle of February, to Pittsburgh in March, and to Los Angeles in April. I have been operating now through the "National Urban Coalition for Peace and Justice." I am one of the three national spokesmen for the organization. The other two are Carl Upchurch and Spike Moss. Carl is out of Ohio and Spike Moss is out of Minneapolis, Minnesota.

*Question: As you move to other cities are there things that you would do differently?*

With African-American mayors we received warm receptions, with White mayors we had cold receptions. In Cleveland the Mayor, the chairman of the City Council, and the Chief of Police supported our efforts to bring peace. In Minneapolis it was just the opposite. In Chicago we had African-American support but Mayor Daley did not support us. In Saint Louis the mayor has invited us again. In Newark the mayor has invited us again. Sometimes I go myself or send others to go and see what religious organizations will support us, so it does not appear to be an outside force coming in but a national force working with the local forces.

*Question: To what extent do people realize your connection with the Hebrew Israelite Community?*

This is an important part of it, because after 20 plus years in Israel, where we were in a very hostile political environment, with Israel representing almost 102 nationalities and eighty two languages spoken in this country. If we as African-Americans were able to come to one of the most volatile pieces of real estate in the world, yet never lift a gun and never be in a physical confrontation with the Jewish citizens or the Arab citizens, then we could bring a message on how to resolve conflict. Second, I always brought a moral position to the table. I argued from a set of principles that would be universally accepted, not only peace and justice. I said to them that prophetically the Kingdom of God was an instrument of peace. I quoted from the Gospels that "blessed are the peacemakers for they shall become the sons of God." I made that a thread everywhere that I went. I was able to organize from a moral standpoint. I could show them that without a budget, without guns, without knives, when serious men and women sat down in truth they could resolve conflict.

One of the things that we did. We brought several of the key gang leaders here to Jerusalem. Some of the brothers are Christian and some under Islam. We brought them here to explain that all of that is one aspect of the faith (monotheism). We brought the leadership to Jerusalem so that they could go back and tell their constituencies that I stood on the top of Mount Zion, I stood on the top of the Dome of the Rock, I stood on the top of the Dome of St. Peter and saw for myself that this is a place where we could bring peace.

I told them that there is no way to undo that this man has killed your brother or this man has killed your sister. What we have to do is have a beginning. I said that if Menachem Begin can sit with Sadat, the Americans can sit with the Japanese after Hiroshima, you cannot tell me that violence cannot be settled. If Rabin and Arafat are willing to talk, you cannot tell me that two African-American youths cannot sit down and talk. So I broadened the base, to give them a perspective for what they were doing.

## An Interview with Ben Ammi Ben Israel (March 1994)

*Question: What role has the community played in mediation in the past, the present, and what is likely for the future?*

One of the things we have found out over the years is that individuals have to have great fortitude for mediation. Those whom you are mediating the issues for, must listen. You find persons willing to mediate, but one of the reasons why mediation does not succeed is that the parties do not listen. This has been the problem between the African-American and the American Jewish community. Over the years, neither side has wanted to listen. The African-Americans did not want to listen because they felt the relationship was paternal. The American Jewish community did not want to listen because they felt that they would have to concede what they felt was their lofty position.

We feel that we are in a very unique position since we have Jewish nationality, we bring the spiritual aspect to the occasion. We have lived in Israel now for 24 years. We know the Jewish community much better than the average African-American and as well as those in positions of leadership. We know the African-American community because our roots are there.

I spoke with the presidents of the American Jewish organizations on my visit to the States. I listened to them. I had not been to the States in 23 years. They did not really know me and I did not know them. It was the same with the African-American community. I did not want to take any strong positions, but listen. I spoke to the major African-American organizations. I was trying to stimulate them to form a clear picture of their position. Although I had some gut feelings, I did not want to appear to have come with pre-conceived ideas about the issues. I felt it was a successful journey (1993). I felt that I came to know all of the players. The interviews equipped me to play a role in a problem that has reached crisis proportions.

I explained to the leaders of each community that there are two kinds of fighters: He that fights because he likes to fight and he that fights to win. I said to some of the African-American leaders that we are trying to win a struggle of redemption. There is a way you have to go about this. If you are to remain an American, you must consider the parameters in which you have to operate, and you must define the victory. I asked lay persons: "What defines the victory for you? I do not think you know. You seem to just want to antagonize whites and Jewish people. What do you want? Is higher education what you want? Then since the 1930s, certainly you have achieved a higher level of education. If that was the objective it has been achieved. If you keep on complaining, you just antagonize people. It is the same for economic development. You are the tenth wealthiest nation in the world. You won. Why do you want to antagonize people." I wanted them to understand that they were simply doing things without any objectives. I wanted to make them understand that their leaders had left them in a vacuum.

We had our own problems in Israel between the community and the Israeli government. We demonstrated in Washington, D.C. and in Jerusalem. But we had an objective. We wanted dialogue. When the dialogue began the demonstration was over. I was not doing this because I wanted to, but because we had an objective. In the US the parties involved do not know what they want from each other. There was no solution to their problem because there were no objectives nor goals. Those in positions of leadership were simply doing things for their own personal objectives.

This was creating a platform for mediation. Once they understand their goals, we could begin to mediate. During the next season we will be able to play a major role in the African-American community and with the American Jewish community. The problems spill over into Israel. We have been placed by the God of creation in a very unique position to bring these two antagonists together. We must always inject the God element, the righteous element, in negotiation. We may receive another invitation. I feel that we will.

*Question: You can relate to the various groups of people involved in these conflicts. This is traditional mediation. But you seem to be doing much more. You are mediating between man and nature, man and the environment. The environment cannot speak for itself. Unless you understand the cycles of nature, you cannot speak for nature. Nature is surrounded by the idea of the righteous life. But God does not speak directly. The word comes through people. So all of these are the same. Are some of the same sensitivities needed to understand the needs of people, the relation to the environment, and the relation to God and the righteous life?*

I think that you have expressed it very eloquently. The prophets have told us that the entire world has been deceived. The entire world is rotating on the axis of a lie. The body does not just age and die. It has to be programmed to destruct, to deteriorate and die. So there must be an anti-life force on the planet. An anti-life mentality. Unless someone explains, people will not know that they should change their mind set. So we are mediating between man and the

Creator. Between man and nature. Nature and God are essentials if you are going to experience life. This brings us back to the power to define. You ask people what is life. They cannot tell you what life is. Their life is all based on materialistic values. So the more materials they obtain, the better they feel their lives will be. But is that really life. If not, what is the true wealth.

Someone is giving us the impression that nature is expendable. If there is a lie, then at some point you have to stop and challenge the lie. The drowning man may not appreciate the blow you have to give him to save his life. The God of life understood that he had to give the individual a hard blow to save him. The drowning man cannot save himself. Sometimes you have to say harsh things, to reveal harsh realities. In our world, people have been guided away from God. We read that the last dominion of the Euro-Gentile was to be an economic dominion. There was to be an economic superpower. It would succeed in deifying money. Today we find that it is the almighty dollar, the almighty yen, the almighty pound. Money determines life. With money people feel that there is nothing that they cannot do. Without money they feel that there is nothing that they can do. Their lives depend upon money. Money has supplanted God as the giver of life.

This transformation has taken place very subtly. Money has been deified. It determines how happy you are. It determines your friends, it determines your enemies. All of those attributes were once attributed to God. We must take a position and try to mediate again. To try to bring men back to God. The difference between a political struggle and a redemptive struggle is that in politics you attempt to use politics to obtain economics to provide better social conditions. When you attempt to guide the people back unto God, the objective is to come to oneness with God. You cannot win a political struggle. The ultimate victory has to be won through a redemptive struggle. Politics are not absolute. Only when you deal with God can you deal with the absolute. Consider homosexuality and abortion, in the United States the opinion on these issues varies with whether Republicans or Democrats are in power. Politics is good and evil. It is unstable in all of its ways. There is no absolute. The individual is divided against himself. You can only accept an absolute when you return unto God.

Is there a God? There is no absolute until you accept God. Life is diametrically opposed to death. Without God people can never experience true life. The insurance policy and burial policy are part of the programming. All of the cells in your body are eavesdropping on your mind. They are controlled by your mind. No layman controls his own destiny. Destiny is something you cannot avoid. The destiny of a man is controlled by his character which is programmed by his mind. I am trying to take control of a people's destiny. I am trying to take control of their lives. I am asked, who are you to force yourself upon people? But someone has already forced themselves upon you. Your heart attack started some years ago when you were told that "Big Mac" was good. I want to guide people back to the destiny that God desires for them. No sickness, no disease, one family. So we have the same understanding.

Once we came from the same father and mother. Who said there were Red men and Brown men, and Black men? They all came from one father and one mother. But as they grew up they wanted to deny their Black father and mother. The commandment says "Honor thy father and thy mother." As nations turn away from their original father and mother, they must die. This is a redemptive struggle. Politics lets us believe what we want to believe.

We must keep our relationship with God intact. We must keep our origins intact. Otherwise we think that we are living but we have never experienced true life. People feel uncomfortable with prophets and saviors. To mediate between man and God is a redemptive plan. But a price must be paid. Sometimes certain people are anointed, who must walk through the valley of the shadow of death. But for the love of God, people suffer these things. What I do is an expression of my love for humanity. We share this truth. It is not just centered around the African-American.

How do you listen to nature and God in order to play the mediating role? The first thing is that you must recategorize nature and see plants as living organisms. The ancient cultures had holidays such as succot. The people had to bring the first fruits to the temple, to the priest. You would lift them up. Was that a ritual or a high-level of respect that men had for plants? It was a reminder of the high-level of respect that plants once had in our lives. You have an entire generation of children that have not even walked on the dirt.

They have never experienced shelling a pea, picking the grapes. They do not understand that nature is life, that in nature there are living organisms. Nature is not just something to look good. It is not seen as a part of us that we depend upon. Over history, man has remained basically agrarian. We have had dynasties and other great institutions, but until 100 years ago the planet was basically agrarian. Was that just coincidence. Or did man know that he had to remain closely associated with the soil?

The basic elements are air, fire, water, soil. The sun represents fire. Today you are advised not to lay in the sun. You are told not to drink the water, it is polluted. People do not care about the soil. In Genesis we find the commandment, "every seed to yield after its kind." The orange seed yields an orange, not an apple. How does a pea feel about a young child that does not know to touch it? There is something more to shelling the peas, snapping the beans, and shucking the corn than just preparing a meal.

Over history all people remained closely associated with the four elements on which their lives depended. We have to put the farmers back in the land. We must go out to the field together. Planting and harvesting is a part of life. Before the food provides your nourishment it reveals a God element as it grows from a seed to a plant. Then people will begin to love nature again. Today nature has become their enemy. The tree has to again become the essential provider for the nutrition of man. The Euro-centric dominion has taken man completely away from the elements. Where is the end? What are you going to do with people? Nature is a living part of us. We must intercede to bring people back to nature. To love it and touch it. Every child has to walk out into the field and see the crops.

# Bibliography

Abu-Lughod L. (1990) The romance of resistance: Tracing transformations of power through Bedouin women. In P. R. Sanday and R. G. Goodenough (eds.) *Beyond the second sex*. Philadelphia: University of Pennsylvania Press.

Adelfila, J. A. (1975) *Slave religion in the Antebellum South*. Ph.D. Dissertation, Brandeis University.

Aidala, A. (1985) Social change, gender roles, and new religious movements. *Sociological Analysis*, 46(Fall): 287–314.

Anthony, D., and T. Robbins. (1982) Contemporary religious ferment and moral ambiguity. In E. Barker (ed.) *New religious movements: A perspective for understanding society*. New York: Edwin Mellen Press. pp. 243–262.

Anyon, J. (1983) Intersections of gender and class: Accommodation and resistance by working-class and affluent females to contradictory sex roles. In W. Stephen and L. Barton (eds.), *Gender, class and education*. Sussex, England: The Falmer Press

Baer, H. A., and M. Singer. (1992) *African-American religion in the twentieth century: Varieties of Protest and Accomodation*. Knoxville: University of Tennessee Press.

Bahtyah, E. E. (1994) Divine marriage, keys to marital happiness. Dimona, Israel: Hebrew Israelite Community Publication.

Barker, E. (1982) *New religious movements: A perspective for understanding society*. New York: Edwin Mellen Press.

Barkun, M. (1985) The awakening cycle of controversy. *Sociological Analysis Review*, 6:663–669.

Beckford, J. A. (1985) *Cult controversies: The societal response to religious movements*. London: Tavistock Publications.

Ben Ammi. (1990) *God, the black man, and truth*. Washington, D.C.: Communicators Press.

Ben Ammi. (1991a) *God and the law of relativity*. Washington, D.C.: Communicators Press.

Ben Ammi. (1991b) *The messiah and the end of this world*. Washington, D.C.: Communicators Press.

Ben Ammi. (1994) *Everlasting life.* Washington, D.C.: Communicators Press.

Ben-Yehuda, S. (1975) *Black Hebrew Israelites: From America to the promised land.* New York: Vantage Press.

Bercovitch, J., and J. Z. Rubin. (eds.) (1992) *Mediation in international relations: Multiple approaches to conflict management.* London: Macmillan.

Berger, G. (1978) *Black Jews in America: A documentary with commentary.* New York: Commission on Synagogue Relations, Federation of Jewish Philanthropies of New York.

Berger, P. L. (1963) *Invitation to sociology: A humanist perspective.* New York: Anchor Books.

Berger, P. L., and T. Luckmann. (1967) *The Social construction of reality.* Garden City, NY: Anchor Books.

Bernal, M. (1987) *Black Athena: The Afroasiatic roots of classical civilization. Vol. 1.* New Brunswick, NJ: Rutgers University Press.

Bourdieu, P. (1977) *Outline of a theory of practice.* Cambridge: Cambridge University Press.

Bourguignon, E. (1980) *A world of women.* New York: Bergin Publishers.

Brotz, H. (1964) *The black Jews of Harlem.* New York: Free Press of Glencoe.

Campbell, C. (1982) Some comments on the new spirituality and post industrial society. In E. Barker (ed.), *New religious movements: A perspective for understanding society.* New York: Edwin Mellen Press. pp. 232–241.

Capra, F. (1983) *The turning point.* Toronto: Bantam New Age Books.

Chertok, H. (1991) Kingdom come in Dimona. *Jerusalem Post,* July 12 (Contact):16–18.

Comaroff, J. (1985) *Body of power, spirit of resistance.* Chicago: University of Chicago Press.

Cronon, E. D. (1955) *Black Moses: The story of Marcus Garvey and the United Negro Improvement Association.* Madison, WI: University of Wisconsin Press.

Ferm, V. (ed.) (1945) *Encyclopedia of religion.* New York: Philosophical Library.

Fishkoff, S. (1995) The commandment keepers. *The Jerusalem Post Magazine,* (March 3):8–11.

Foucault, M. (1980) *Power/knowledge: Selected interviews and other writings, 1972–1977.* C. Gordon (ed.). New York: Pantheon.

Gavriel HaGadol, Prince with O. B. Israel (1993) *The impregnable people: An exodus of African Americans back to Africa.* Washington, D.C.: Communicators Press.

Gerber, I. J. (1977) *The heritage seekers: American blacks in search of Jewish identity.* Middle Village, NY: Jonathan David Publishers.

Glass, D. (1980) Ha-Cushim Ha-Ivrim: Din vHeshbon vHamlatzot shel ha-Vadah l'Vdikat Bayot ha-Cushim ha-Ivrim [The Black Hebrews: Report and Recommendations of the Committee to Investigate the Problems of the Black Hebrews]. Jerusalem.

Gramsci, A. (1971) *Selections from prison notebooks.* Q. Hoare and G. Nowell Smith (eds. and trans.). London: Lawrence and Wishart.

Hare, A. P. (1992) Informal mediation by private individuals. In J. Bercovitch and J. Z. Rubin (eds.), *Mediation in international relations*. London: Macmillan. pp. 52–63.

Hare, A. P. (1993a) Small groups in organizations. In R. T. Golembiewski (ed.), *Handbook of organizational behavior*. New York: Marcel Dekker. pp. 61–89.

Hare, A. P. (1993b) Black Hebrews in Israel: Constructing a virtuous reality. Paper presented at the Annual Meeting of the Israeli Anthropological Association, Jerusalem.

Haywood, C. L. (1983) The authority and empowerment of women among spiritualist groups. *Journal for the Scientific Study of Religion* 22:156–166.

Hurston, Z. N. (1984) *Moses: Man of the mountain*. Urbana, IL: University of Illinois Press.

Jenkins, D. (1975) *Black Zion: The return of Afro-Americans and West Indians to Africa*. London: Wildwood House.

Lamphere, L. (1974) Strategies, cooperation and conflict among women in domestic groups. In M. Rosaldo and L. Lamphere (eds.), *Woman, culture and society*. Stanford: Stanford University Press.

Levine, L. W. (1977) *Black culture and black consciousness*. Oxford: Oxford University Press.

Linton, R. (1943) Nativistic movements. *American Anthropologist*, 44:230–240.

Lounds, M. (c.1981) *Israel's Black Jews*. Washington, D.C.: University Press of America.

Mazrui, A. A. (1986) *The Africans: A triple heritage*. Boston: Little, Brown & Co.

McDaniel, A. (1990) The power of culture: A review of the idea of Africa's influence on the family structure in antebellum America. *Journal of Family History*, 15 (2 Apr.):225–238.

McGuire, W. J. (1985) Attitudes and attitude change. In G. Lindzey and E. Aronson (eds.), *Handbook of social psychology*. New York: Random House. pp. 233–346.

Melton, G. (1993) Another look at new religions. *ANNALS, AAPSS*, 527, (May):97–112.

Memmi, A. (1967) [1957] *The colonizer and the colonized*. Boston: Beacon Press.

Monogan, A. (1985) Rethinking matrifocality. *Phylon* 46(4):353–362.

Murphy, Y., and R. Murphy. (1974) *Women of the forest*. New York: Columbia University Press.

O'Dea, T. F. (1968) Sects and cults. In D. L. Sills (ed.), *International encyclopedia of the social sciences*, Vol. 14. New York: Macmillan & Free Press. pp. 130–136.

Palmer, S. (1993) Women's "cocoon work" in new religious movements: Sexual experimentation and feminine rites of passage. *Journal for the Scientific Study of Religion*, 32(4):343–355.

Robbins T., and D. Bromley (1992) Social experimentation and the significance of American new religions: A focussed religious essay. *Research in the Social Scientific Study of Religion*, 4:1–28.

Rose, S. (1987) Women warriors: The negotiation of gender in a charismatic community. *Sociological Analysis*, 48(3):245–258.

Rubin, J. Z. (1981) *Dynamics of third party intervention: Kissinger in the Middle East.* New York: Praeger.

Santamaria, U. (1987) Black Jews: The religious challenge or politics versus religion. *European Journal of Sociology*, 28(2): 217–240.

Scott, J. C. (1985) *Weapons of the weak: Everyday forms of peasant resistance.* New Haven: Yale University Press.

Sherkat, D. E., and C. G. Ellison (1991) The politics of Black religious change: Disaffiliation from Black mainline denominations. *Social Forces* 70(2):431–454.

Singer, M. C. (1979) Saints of the kingdom: Group emergence, individual affiliation and social change among the Black Hebrews of Israel. Ph.D. Dissertation University of Utah.

Singer, M. C. (1988) The social context of conversion to a Black religious sect. *Review of Religious Research,* 30(2):177–191.

Smallwood, D. (1991) The Hebrew Israelite Community: Forging a new black society in God's land. *N'Digo* (Supplement to the *Chicago Sun-Times*). February Black History Month Issue:3–8.

Stack, C. (1974, 1982 pub.) *All our kin, strategies for survival in a black community.* New York: Harper & Row.

Stark, R., and W. S. Bainbridge (1980) Networks of faith: Recruitment to cults and sects. *American Journal of Sociology* 85(6):1376–95.

Straus, R. A. (1979) Religious conversion as a personal and collective accomplishment. *Sociological Analysis* 40:158–165.

*The original African heritage study bible: King James version.* (1993) Nashville, TN: James C. Winston Publishing Co.

Turner, V. (1974) *Dramas, fields, and metaphors: Symbolic action in human society.* Ithaca, NY: Cornell University Press.

Wallace, A. F. C. (1956) Revitalization movements. *American Anthropologist,* 58: 264–281.

Wallis, R. (1985) The dynamics of change in the human potential movement. In R. Stark (ed.) *Religious movements: Genesis, exodus and numbers.* New York: Paragon House Publishers.

Williams, B. F. (1991) *Stains on my name: War in my veins: Guyana and the politics of cultural struggle.* Durham, NC: Duke University Press.

Wilson, B. (ed.) (1967) *Patterns of sectarianism: Organization and ideology in social and religious movements.* London: Heinemann.

Wilson, B. (1970) *Religious sets: A sociological study.* London: World University Library.

Wilson, B. R. (1992) *The social dimensions of sectarianism.* Oxford: Clarendon Press.

Wolf, M. (1985) *Revolution postponed: Women in contemporary China.* Stanford: Stanford University Press.

Wright, S. M. (1992) Women and the charismatic community: Defining the attraction. *Sociological Analysis,* 53:S, S35–S49.

# Name Index

# Subject Index

# About the Contributors

Prince Immanuel Ben Yehuda is a member of the Holy Council, the spiritual guiding body of the African Hebrew Israelites of Jerusalem. He oversees the community's activities in the Northeast United States and serves as their liaison to the U. S. Congress.

A. Paul Hare is a Professor of Sociology, Emeritus, at the Department of Behavioral Sciences, Ben-Gurion University, Beer Sheva, Israel and a member of the Social Studies Center at the Blaustein Institute for Desert Research.

Yadah Baht Israel is a Crowned Sister and serves as a representative for the Hebrew Israelite Community.

Fran Markowitz is a Senior Lecturer in Anthropology in the Department of Behavioral Science, Ben-Gurion University, Israel.

Hagit Peres is a graduate student in the Department of Social Work, Ben-Gurion University, Israel.